MUSICAL INSTRUMENTS, HISTORIC, RARE AND UNIQUE

First published 1921
This edition published by Lector House in 2025

ISBN: 978-93-6138-237-6

Lector House LLP
Registered Office: H. No. 96, Block C, Tomar Colony,
Burari, Delhi – 110084, India
info@lectorhouse.com
www.lectorhouse.com

MUSICAL INSTRUMENTS, HISTORIC, RARE AND UNIQUE

ALFRED JAMES HIPKINS

2025

LECTOR HOUSE LLP

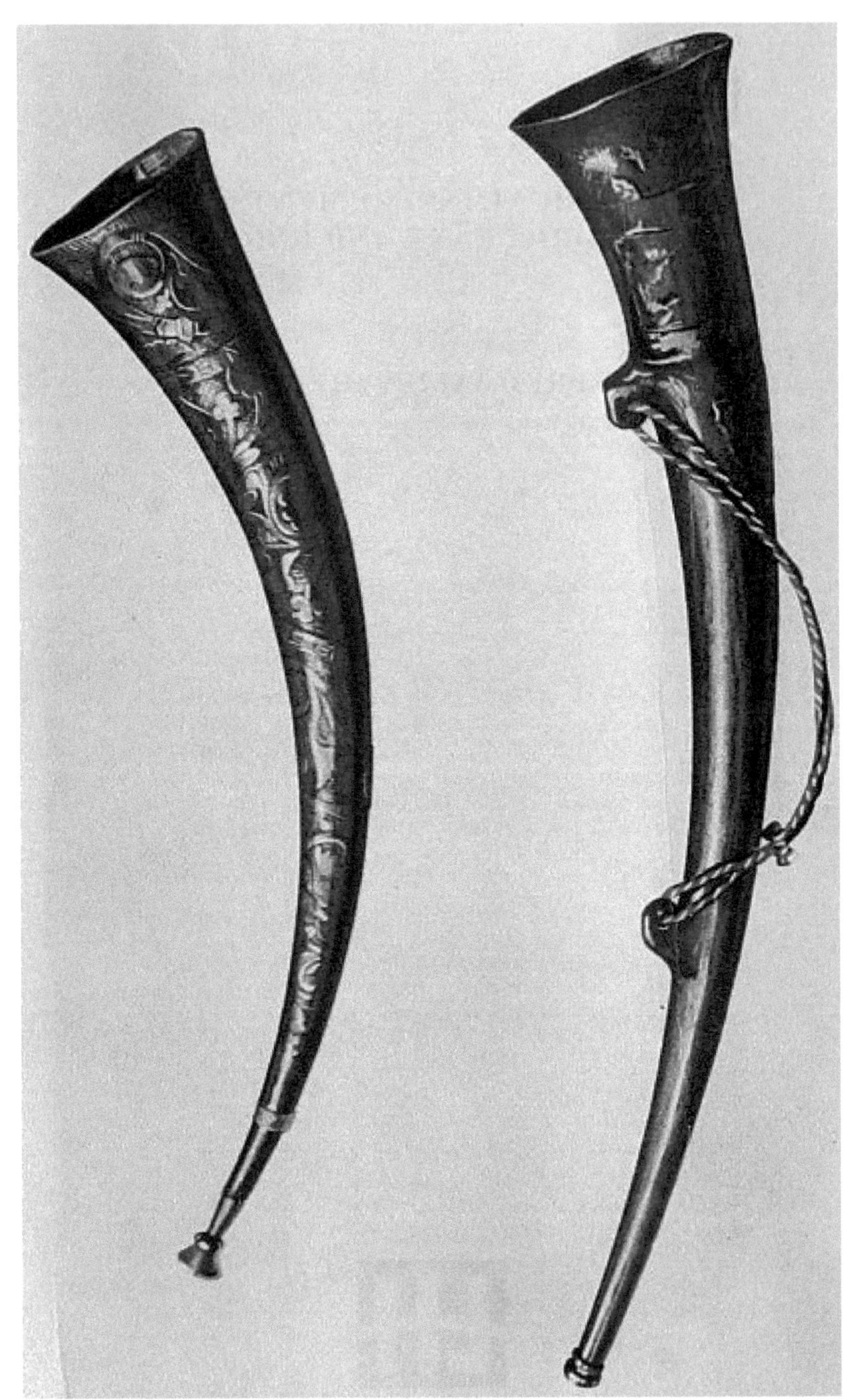

Plate I.

MUSICAL INSTRUMENTS HISTORIC, RARE AND UNIQUE

THE SELECTION, INTRODUCTION AND DESCRIPTIVE NOTES

BY

A. J. HIPKINS, F. S. A. LOND.

AUTHOR OF THE ARTICLE "PIANOFORTE"
IN THE ENCYCLOPÆDIA BRITANNICA

ILLUSTRATED BY
A SERIES OF FORTY-EIGHT PLATES IN COLOURS
DRAWN BY WILLIAM GIBB

The Woodcuts at the head of this page (from the British Museum) represent Sir Michael Mercator, of Venloo, Musical Instrument Maker to King Henry VIII.

CONTENTS

INTRODUCTION.

T is claimed for this book, intended to illustrate rare historical and beautiful Musical Instruments, that it is unique. Classical, Mediæval, Japanese, and other varieties of Decorative Art, Weapons, and Costumes, have found worthy illustration and adequate description, but hitherto no attempt has been made to represent in a like manner the grace and external charm of fine lutes and harps, of viols, virginals, and other instruments. Engravings have been produced, in historical or technical works; but the greater number of these are mere repetitions continued from one to the other, and have no specially æsthetic interest. Beauty of form and fitness of decoration demand more than the commonplace homage paid to simple use, and while we should never lose sight of the purpose of a musical instrument, its capacity to produce agreeable and various sounds, we can take advantage of its form and material, and, making it lovely to look upon, give pleasure to the eye as well as the ear. It is hardly necessary to say that the love of adornment or ornament is an attribute of the human race. It is to be found everywhere and in every epoch when life is, for the time being, safe and the means of existence secure. Some favourite manner of decoration is the characteristic stamp of a people, a period, or a country. The earliest monuments we can point to that represent musical instruments, show a tendency to adorn them or to place them with decorative surroundings. The Egyptians, the Assyrians, the ancient Greeks supply a record that has been continued by the Persians and Saracens, in the Gothic age and the Renaissance, always repeating, as it were, in an ineffaceable script, the precept that the hand should minister to the gratification of the eye, and satisfy it by alternating excitement with repose. And so it was, until the marvellous mechanical advance in the present century has not only caused us to forget, by its overwhelming power, what our predecessors so steadfastly continued, but has induced us to regard the ugly as sufficient if the mere practical end is served. By thus chilling the appreciation and pursuit of decorative invention, that faculty has been numbed for the time being, and there is danger of its being lost altogether. It may be answered that real artistic work is occasionally done, and there are examples of it to be found in musical instruments; a good organ case is sometimes made, sometimes a fine decoration for a piano case. If there is any hope of an awakening of the love for musical instruments that finds expression in their adornment, its promise lies in the beautiful designs that have been, of late years, so meritoriously carried out for pianos—the invention of Mr. Alma Tadema, Mr. Burne Jones, Mr. Fox, and Miss Kate Faulkner. Good decoration need not be a privilege of the rich; the old Antwerp clavecin-makers, who were all members of the guild of St. Luke, the artists' guild, knew how to worthily decorate their instruments at little cost, as may be seen in the Ruckers Virginal, Plate XVIII. They painted their sound-boards with appropriate ornamentation, and used bright colour to heighten the effect of their instruments when open. The Italians went even farther in richer details, and beautified other stringed instruments besides those with key-boards. The persistence of noble traditions is shown in the exquisite ornament of the Siamese instruments (Plates XLII. and XLIII.) and of the Japanese Koto (Plate XLVI.). It would be grievous if this Eastern inheritance were lost through the engrafting of Western ideas and reception of our material civilisation. The incentive to all such work is the pleasure found in it, and without pleasure in work the life of the worker is aimless and sad.

In describing musical instruments we can refer to no beginnings; those that may be discerned dimly in the glimmering of the historic dawn present a certain completeness that marks an intellectual advance already accomplished. The well-known Egyptian Nefer, a spade-like guitar, or rather tamboura, invited by its long neck the stopping of various notes upon its strings. As early as the Third Dynasty, it had already been so long in use as to have become incorporated in the pictorial language of the Hieroglyphics, in which its representation presented the concept or symbol of the attribute *good*. This stringed instrument, thus complex in its playing, must have been already grey with age when it was cut in stone in the monument of the beautiful Princess Nefer-t, now in the museum at Bulaq. We cannot conjecture when it was discovered that more tones than one could be got from a single string by taking advantage of the expedient of a long neck or finger-board, or from a single pipe by boring lateral holes in it, and closing those holes to produce different notes with the fingers. Even these remote inventions, certainly prehistoric, seem to require that there should be yet older inventions—those which placed pipes or strings of different lengths, or strings of the same length but of different thicknesses and tension, side by side, as in the syrinx or Pan's pipes, or the harp and lyre.

The late Carl Engel, *Music of the Most Ancient Nations* (London, 1864), has formed a kind of Development theory for musical instruments, giving the earliest place to the drum, and the latest to the stringed instruments; those of the latter with key-boards having been invented almost in our own time. This theory has lately been reconstructed upon a more scientific basis by Mr. Rowbotham (*History of Music*, vol. i., London, 1885). The drum and tambourine, and other clashing and mere time-marking instruments, as sistrums, cymbals, castagnettes, and triangles, are on the limit of musical sound and noise, inclining, for the most part, to the latter. The drum is widely used in religious services in different parts of the world, and to play the sistrum was in ancient Egypt the prerogative of a high order of priesthood. The various Buddhist gongs resemble the kettledrums in this respect, that they have a more definable musical element in them, and we find these sonorous metal instruments widely used in China and the Indo-Chinese countries, in Java, and the Indian Archipelago. The Indian drums (Plate XLI.), according to the theory just mentioned, should be aboriginal, but the most ancient, the M'ridang, is attributed to the god S'iva, and is therefore Aryan. Her Majesty the Queen's State

Kettledrum (Plate XXXV.) here adorned with a richly embroidered silk banneret, serves to show the highest point the drum has yet attained in estimation and use. On a much higher level is that arrangement of wooden or metal bars in those instruments classed generally as Harmonicons, which are especially at home in Java, Siam, and Burma, and are known to be used from the Hill country of India in the one direction, to Africa in the other. The beautiful Siamese Ranat and Khong (Plate XLIII.) and the Zulu Marimba (Plate XLVIII.) are examples of this wide distribution, and in the latter the gourd resonators attached to the bars show the simplest form of sound reinforcers, which, perfected in various Eastern instruments, such as the Indian Vínas and Sitárs (Plate XL.) has in Europe attained its crowning artistic development in the beautiful pear-shaped Resonance bodies of the Lute and Mandoline. We find also varieties of this beautiful form in the Georgian and Turcoman tambouras, the Colascione of Southern Italy and similar instruments, the migrations of which may here and there be traced along the lines of religious movements, as in Central Asia and Hindostan, in China, the Corea, and Japan. For instance, the shorter-necked lutes and guitars, the rebec, rebab, and other precursors of the viols and violins, which, borrowed from the Arabic population of the Holy Land, actually came to Europe upon the reflex wave of the Crusades. The Saracenic occupation of Spain had, however, its share in the transmission of these instruments, and of a taste for the *pizzicato,* and also of an elaboration of vocal and instrumental ornament, which has remained in the popular airs and dances of that country, and, an important characteristic of the music of the Troubadours and Trouvères, has left its mark upon our modern music everywhere. The Arab blood in Spain may have tended to preserve the use of the guitar as a national instrument in that country. A Guitar (Plate XXIX.) and a Cetera (Plate XXVIII.) made by Stradivarius, as he usually signed his name, are of especial interest as showing that he was not above making more simple instruments than violins. The beautiful tortoiseshell Guitar (Plate X.) has a tradition that connects it with Mary of Scots and the unfortunate Rizzio. In all these guitar and lute instruments, the roses in the sound-boards show a wealth of invention in design that is truly astonishing. A work of this kind would not be without interest if it were devoted only to these roses, and to those of spinets and harpsichords. Guitars have flat backs, and lutes shell or pear-shaped resonance bodies, and the former are again divided into the guitar proper with catgut strings, and cithers with wire strings necessitating the employment of a plectrum. The Cetera is the Italian name of the cither, and the one drawn in Plate XIV. is of remarkable, although not unusual, beauty. The cither to which the name of Queen Elizabeth is traditionally attached, belongs to the English family of the Pandore, Orpheoreon, and Penorcon; it is not exactly one of these instruments, but it most nearly resembles the last named. As a fine specimen of English work, in no way ceding to the Italian, this beautiful instrument, commonly known as Queen Elizabeth's Lute (Plate IX.), cannot be too highly extolled. The description accompanying this drawing, and in fact the descriptions of all the drawings, must be referred to for those special particulars that are more conveniently given separately. The Lute (Plate XV.) is one of the finest existing examples of its kind. It bears the label of Vvendelio Venere, Padua, dated 1600, and marks the culmination of that once most favourite instrument. The large bass lutes—the theorboes and chitarroni—that came into use about that date, were rendered necessary through the weakness in the bass of the contemporary harpsichord, which was insufficient as a sub-structure for the Continuo, or Thorough Bass, intended to accompany the Recitativo, then recently introduced at Florence, and forming an essential part of that Monody that was the latest blooming of the Renaissance, as applied to the latest art, harmonised music. The Venetian Theorboes (or Tiorbe) and Chitarroni (Plates XVI. and XXI.) are of great beauty and historical interest. But the lute, even when diapasons or extra bass strings were added to it, went out, being superseded by the more useful, although less beautifully toned, spinet. The latest lute instruments are the pleasing Mandolines to which fashion may possibly grant a new lease of popularity. These instruments are drawn in Plate XXIII. Both ear and eye are equally gratified in that culmination of qualities attained in a violin, in which the sound and shape are so intimately and inseparably connected that we fail to conceive the one without some mental reference to the other. The form and colour of a fine violin are in themselves so beautiful that it seems scarcely possible to enhance their effect by adding any kind of decoration, but in Plate XXV. it will be seen that Antonio Stradivari, with whom the instrument reached perfection, has successfully inlaid one of his masterpieces with an appropriate design. Another violin by the same illustrious master, in this instance without adornment, is drawn in Plate XXVI. The particular characteristics of another famous Cremona maker, Giuseppe Guarneri, who signed himself "Del Gesù," and is accounted Stradivari's only rival, are also illustrated in this plate. With forty-eight plates, however, to which this work is limited, no complete scheme can be offered of the rich varieties of musical instruments that exist, but the pictorially interesting Viola d'Amore (Plate XXVII.) and the Viola da Gamba (Plate XIX.) have not been overlooked.

Wind instruments, although they may be of earlier invention in their rudimentary forms than those with strings, as in the old-world fable of Apollo and Marsyas, are always placed second. But they have an equal interest intrinsically and historically, and like drums and gongs, have an especial connection with the sacred rites of various nations. The Jewish Shophar, a simple ram's horn, a woodcut of which, drawn from an interesting example preserved at the great Synagogue, Aldgate, London, figures at the end of this Introduction, is the oldest wind instrument in present use in the world. It is first named in the Bible as sounding when the Lord descended upon Mount Sinai, and there seems to be little doubt that it has been continuously used in the Mosaic Service from the time it was established until now. It is sounded in the synagogues at the New Year and on the Fast of the Day of Atonement. The Talmud gives ten reasons for sounding the Shophar at the New Year, which may be summed up as reminding those who hear it of the Creation, Penitence, and the Law, of the Prophets, who were as watchmen blowing trumpets, of the Temple and the Binding of Isaac, of Humility, the gathering together of Israel, the Resurrection, and the day of Judgment, when the trumpet shall sound for all. The embouchure of the Shophar is very difficult, and but three proper tones are usually obtained from it, although in some instances higher notes can be got. The short rhythmic flourishes are common, with unimportant differences, to both the German and Portuguese Jews, and consequently date from before their separation.

These flourishes as used in the Ritual are the Tekiah (T'qiȧh)  Shebarim (Sh'bharim)  and Teruah (T'ruȧh) usually a tongued *vibrato* of the lower note. The Gedolah  is the great Tekiah concluding the flourishes. The shophar is usually a ram's horn flattened by heat, the bore being a cylindrical tube of very small calibre, which opens into a kind of bell of parabolic form. The notes here given are those usually produced, but from the empirical formation of the embouchure and a peculiarity of the player's lips, an octave is occasionally produced instead of the normal fifth. The fundamental, if obtained, is not regarded as a true shophar note. Through the mediation of a friend, whose assistance has enabled me to gather this information, I have heard the shophar flourishes played by a competent performer, and am enabled to give an authoritative notation of these strangely interesting historical phrases, for the final correction of which I have to thank the Rev. Francis Cohen.

Bronze horns are also of very ancient use, and existing specimens, chiefly of Celtic or Scandinavian origin, are frequently richly ornamented. Their employment appears to have been for war, for hunting, and the feast. In more recent times, their possession has been attached to feudal customs, as the transfer and holding of land, and at last through the growth of large cities they became associated, as the interesting Dover and Canterbury Horns (Plate I.) were, with municipal customs. Horns were sounded for the curfew, and an especially characteristic example of such horn-blowing is a dramatic feature introduced by Wagner at the close of the second act of his Shakespearean Music Drama, *Die Meistersinger von Nürnberg*. Earl Spencer's very beautiful ivory horn or Oliphant (Plate VII.) was most likely intended for the chase. Of other simple wind instruments depending upon the player's lips, the ancient Roman Lituus and Buccina (Plate XXXVII.) are eminently interesting examples. The Roman horse-soldier bore the Lituus, so called from its resemblance to an Augur's staff, and the foot-soldier, the Tuba and circular Buccina. They marched to the sound of instruments, the tones of which were produced exactly as they are in the trumpet and bugle we are familiar with—from the vibration of the lips, varying with the pressure and force of wind within a cup-like mouthpiece. These tones, being from natural harmonics, are not different now from what they were when Cæsar first landed in Britain, or, indeed, the first notes from a horn that were ever produced. Of modern brass instruments drawn, there are two possessing historical interest—the Cavalry Bugle in Plate XXXVI. which belongs to H.R.H. the Prince of Wales, and sounded the moonlight charge of the Household Cavalry at Kassassin in Egypt, and a trumpet that sounded the famous charge at Salamanca. By way of contrast there is the silver State Trumpet (Plate XXXV.), one of ten that were employed in peaceful service for Her Majesty Queen Victoria during her long and gracious rule.

The Syrinx, or Pan's pipes, has been already referred to, and may be described as composed of a certain number of flute-pipes, the sounds being produced by directing the breath against the sharp edge of each pipe. Plato considered the use of the Syrinx lawful in rural life, but he condemned the more richly-toned flute. The shepherd's pipe belongs to the Oboe family, inasmuch as it is sounded by means of a reed, an artifice of great antiquity. We do not know anything about its early development, but Chaldean shepherds played upon similar instruments nearly 2000 years ago, while watching their flocks by night, and Neapolitan peasants still play, in memory of those shepherds, upon similar rustic reed pipes, the Zampogna or Cennamella, for nine days preceding the great Church festivals of the Madonna Immaculata and the Nativity. These primitive oboes must be of very great antiquity. It is probable, the shepherd's pipe was at first a smaller reed inserted in a larger one, or the larger one was slit for a reed vibrator, as boys cut them now. The lowland Scotch shepherd's pipe is made of horn, the cover for the reed being also horn. The principle of a reservoir of air to furnish a supply for pipes, the primitive conception of the organ, was known to the Romans and the original form of bagpipe was the Tibia Utricularis. In course of time no instrument was more popular throughout Europe than the bagpipe. Varieties of it (Plates IV. and V.), including specimens of the Cornemuse and Musette, show the modern forms of this now despised instrument. The principle of the drone-bass, common to the Bagpipe and Hurdy-gurdy (Plate XXX.), must have been of universal acceptance in Europe before the knowledge of counterpoint became general. The peculiar scale of intervals of the great Highland bagpipe adds much to what is characteristic in the tones of the instrument. Its divergence of intonation may be due to the incompetency of the instrument-maker to determine the true distances for boring the lateral holes. If so, we must be lenient with him, for even now, with our perfection of mechanical appliances, the boring is not above question. But, of course, accuracy is more nearly attained than it has been at any previous time, even the earlier years of the present century. Another and a more attractive hypothesis for the Highland bagpipe scale, derives its mean or neuter thirds, neither major nor minor, from a Syrian scale, still found at Damascus, and attributes its presence in Europe to the pipes having been brought, like rebecs, rebabs, and lutes, by returning Crusaders, whose wondering admiration for Saracenic Art is well known. It seems scarcely likely that the music would not also have touched them, possessed as it was of a special charm due to ages of Persian and Arabic cultivation. There is abundant evidence in the present day as to the favour shown in the East for those indefinite thirds, which may originate from an ideally equal scale of seven intervals of the same extent, such as the Siamese accept, instead of five of larger and two of smaller, such as obtains with us; or they may be due to an alteration in tuning the lute, attributed by the Arabian philosopher Al Fārābi to a lutenist named Zalzal, who changed one of the frets of the lute to obtain it. It is not necessary to do more than refer to the peculiarities of these Eastern divisions of the scale or the possible survival of one in the Highland bagpipe; the inquirer will find information carried to the limits of our present knowledge in *Recherches sur l'Histoire de la Gamme Arabe, par* J.P.N. Land (Leyden, 1884), and *On the Musical Scales of Various Nations,* by Alexander J. Ellis, a paper read before the London Society of Arts, and published in that Society's Journal, 27th March, 1885. It is sufficient to add that while the neuter third remains a favourite interval in some Eastern countries, as far as investigation has been possible it is known in Europe only among the mountains and in the bagpipe music of the Scottish Gael. The latest development of flute and reed pipes is to be found in the flute, oboe, clarinet, and bassoon of the modern orchestra. Plates XXXVIII. and XXXIX. represent instruments that have been the immediate precursors of or are identical with the instruments named. One, the Dolciano or Tenoroon with a clarinet reed, is of unusual importance as possibly anticipating the invention of the Saxophone. It would require a volume to describe the transformations wind instruments have undergone in the present century, particularly that of the Flute by the late Theobald Boehm. The clarinet and oboe have been less altered because the completely refashioned instruments that have been intended to replace them, the saxophone and the sarrusophone, have not retained those special qualities of tone colour required for the palette of the orchestral composer. But for the brass instruments there has been as yet no halting-place. Furnished early in this century with keys, that important revolution was succeeded by another no less complete—the introduction of the valve or piston system, the gain of which, now almost universally acknowledged, has been largely taken advantage of by Wagner and other recent composers.

The familiar Organ is shown in the Positive and Portable organs (l'orgue positif et portatif), small instruments representing reduced front portions of the Montre, the visible speaking pipes of the mediæval church organ, which was neither more nor less than a large mixture register; that is to say, each key when put down sounded the octave, twelfth, super-octave, and other notes simultaneously with the fundamental note. The movement of the Plain Song, or of any melody with this harmonic structure upon it, was in progressions that no modern musically trained ear could tolerate. Not more than one key of the large church organ could, however, be put down by either hand, as the keys were as broad as the palm, and to press one down required an attack with the player's fist. But the keys of the Portable organ, a processional instrument, were narrow—one hand manipulating the bellows while the player touched the keys with the other. The positive was a chapel or chamber organ, intended to be stationary, and also with narrow keys, admitting of the grasp of an octave. The key-board shown in the Van Eyck St. Cecilia panel of the famous altar-piece at Ghent—the Adoration of the Lamb—has already the complete arrangement of chromatic keys, exactly as in our modern key-board instruments. The date of this panel could not have been later than A.D. 1426. Among the numerous portable organs depicted in paintings of earlier date, the addition of the *ficti,* as the chromatic notes were called, excepting perhaps the B flat, or the B flat and E flat, does not appear. The B flat, however, was not a chromatic, but an essential note in the ecclesiastical scale. Another early instance in a painting by Hans Memling, preserved in the Hospital of St. John at Bruges, is subsequent in date to the Ghent altar-piece, but is still within the fifteenth century. The chromatic keys are here put farther back than in our usual key-boards, as they were also in the fourteenth-century Halberstadt organ. The fourteenth-century portable organ drawn in *Critical and Bibliographical Notes on Early Spanish Music,* by Don Juan F. Riaño (Quaritch, London), 1887, p. 127, shows the B flat only, and figured as an upper key, apparently not raised, but level with the natural keys, which agrees with contemporary representations of the instrument by Fra Angelico. The Portable Organ (Plate XIII.) here drawn is of comparatively late date, these small instruments having remained in use until after the Reformation. The Positive Organ (Plate XI.) is of earlier date, and is so far developed as to have registers and drawstops to govern them; in this example they are an octave apart, but an unimpeachable authority, Praetorius, speaks of a register in a positive organ a fifth from the fundamental one! Our ancestors were evidently not affected by a progression of fifths as we are.

The Regal (Plate XII., and as Bible Regal, Plate XIII.), was equally a part of the old church organ taken out and played by itself. It is the beating-reed register, so called because the reed overlaps its frame, and when vibrating produces a more or less jarring or strident quality of tone. As the free reed does not touch its frame it is less harsh in quality. But the latter variety of reed is of very recent introduction into Europe. Strangely enough, it has been taken from a Chinese mouth organ of great antiquity, the Shêng! This Chinese instrument has seventeen sounding pipes, each furnished with a small brass or copper free reed, and is usually sounded by drawing in the wind, not blowing, being in this respect followed by the present American organ. The adoption in Europe of the principle of the Shêng was due to an application of it at St. Petersburg by an organ-builder named Kirsnick, about 1780, and the enthusiastic advocacy of the Abbé Vogler. (Sir George Grove's *Dictionary of Music and Musicians,* Art. "Vogler," by the Rev. J.H. Mee.) From it are derived our accordion and concertinas, harmonium and American organ, as well as sundry musical toys. The Shêng is drawn in Plate XLIV. It is familiar in Japan, with some variation, as the Sho, and a larger instrument on the same principle used in the Lao States of Siam is there called Phān. In nearly all instances it is retained as a solo instrument. The Siamese musicians, whom H.M. the King of Siam very generously sent at his own expense to the London Inventions Exhibition, and who performed there, in the music room and in the Royal Albert Hall, had among them a Phān player, who always played alone.

Harp-like instruments, but with resonance bodies beneath the strings, appear in their oldest, but a yet highly developed form, in the Chinese Ch'in, or Scholar's Lute. The Japanese Sono Koto (Plate XLVI.) is derived from a modification of the Ch'in, known in China as the Sê, the difference being that while the Ch'in has fixed bridges and a system of stopping, the Sê, and consequently the Koto, have movable bridges and no stops. The Koto is tuned according to the five notes in the octave system that prevails in Japan and, with a difference in the division of the scale, in China, named, by the late Carl Engel, pentatonic. The player kneels upon the ground beside the instrument, and resting or sitting upon his heels, touches the shorter lengths of the strings, as divided by the bridges, with plectra on the thumb and first two fingers, but, at the same time, makes constant use of the longer lengths to press upon or relieve the strings so as to alter the tension and produce intermediate tones. The Koto drawn is one of great beauty. The four characteristic popular instruments of Japan are the Koto, the Siamisen, the Biwa, and the Kokiu (see Plates XLVI. and XLVII.) The Siamisen is allied to the Chinese San-hsien and the Biwa to the Chinese P'i-p'a (see Plate XLIV.). The very curious Siamese Ta'khay, or crocodile (Plate XLIII.), is of the same genus as the Koto and Ch'in, but has been changed into its present form by Siamese ingenuity, which has found a rich field for employment in the decoration of musical instruments, the Siamese, in this respect, bearing the palm in the East, as the Italians have done in the West.

As to the principle of the harp or rather of the psaltery embodied in these parallel strung instruments, it differs from the Egyptian and Assyrian conceptions, which placed the resonance bodies of their harps in a curved disposition, the one below, the other above the strings. Greek lyres had their sound bodies directly underneath the strings. The origin of the Greek lyre is unknown, the name not being Hellenic; it may possibly have been Asiatic, but was not originally Egyptian. It would solve an interesting problem could we know what was the Hebrew kinnor, the harp of the Authorised Version, the most prominent stringed instrument occurring in the richest collection of sacred poetry the world has known, the Hebrew Psalms. Dr. Stainer, who has made a complete analysis of the text, has not got beyond conjecture. It is only certain that the kinnor was a stringed instrument. It is recorded that it was made by Tubal Cain, played upon by Laban the Syrian and by the shepherd boy David. It is mentioned in the Book of Job, and the captive Hebrews in Babylon hung their kinnors on the trees. Whether with or without finger-board, whether a lyre, a trigonon, or a harp, its tones had power over the feelings to produce similar effects to those with which music touches us now, as surely as that the physical law of sympathetic vibration was as active then in Syria, or by the waters of Babylon, as it is to-day in Edinburgh or London.

The forms of Harp drawn in this work (Plates II., III., and XXXIV.) differ from the ancient harps which had no forearm or front pillar, and could therefore have endured but little strain. Yet an old Celtic monument represents a harp-like instrument with this Eastern peculiarity. The extremely interesting Celtic harps here drawn, the Queen Mary and the Lamont harps, have forearms or bows of a constructive strength that would, with the rest of the framing, bear a considerable draught of wire. The Celts and Germanic nations appear to have long cultivated the harp. The word itself is German, but the Celtic people of these islands have different names for it, according to whether they are of the Gaelic or Cymric branch. The common Gaelic name was Cruit (Crot), which comes from a root meaning vibration, but this name has been superseded by Clarsach, which is derived from the resounding board. The Welsh name, Telyn, implies strain or tension. It must be remembered that the triple-strung Welsh Harp is a comparatively modern instrument, and so also is the Welsh Crwth (Plate XXIV.), in the only form in which it has come down to us, as a bowed instrument with extra strings off the finger-board, a peculiarity belonging to the theorbo and lyra-viol. The origin of the Crwth would appear to have been the classical lyre submitted to changes that had come with time, and, as the Continental Rote or Rotta, it was a very common form of instrument in the Middle Ages. It had to give way before Eastern stringed instruments, such as the rebec and lute. The Vína (Plate XL.) is the characteristic Hindu stringed instrument, and has a great antiquity attributed to it. The string is theoretically said to be divided into twenty-two small intervals in the octave, of equal extent, called *s'ruti*, by which the tones and semitones are determined; but recent observation shows that the Hindus are satisfied with a division of twelve semitones in the octave—in fact, our chromatic scale. Smaller intervals are only used for grace notes, and are produced by deflecting the string. Gourd resonators have been mentioned as of probably very ancient use, and the employment of sympathetic strings, in vogue in Europe only in the seventeenth and eighteenth centuries, may be added as also of remote origin in India. The Hindus and Persians have both used gourds attached to the Vínas and Sitárs (Plate XL.) for resonance. In Southern India, where the use of the original Hindu Vína prevails, although the scale now used is at least heptatonic, there is still a leaning towards pentatonic forms of melody. The accordances are in fourths or fifths and octaves. The Sitár of Northern India and greater use of the interval of the third may be attributed to Persian introduction; but throughout India, and more intensely in the south, music is felt as a poetic art, and has a development in its own way, that still remains unrecognised in Europe, although we now have scholars from whose researches and zeal this ignorance may be in time, at least partially, dispelled. Music is acutely felt as a means of expression in India unknown in China or among the Indo-Chinese races.

The vexed question of the introduction of the bow to stringed instruments, upon which the most eminent authorities are not yet disposed to agree, is one that needs only to be mentioned here. Whether of Asiatic or European introduction, it would appear at first to have been only one of the ways by which sounds could be drawn from strings, and that it gradually became victorious over the plectrum, with instruments of the viol kind, which thereby gained a great development. It is even now permitted to use the fingers to a bowed instrument in the *pizzicato* of the violin and violoncello.

The Psaltery was a plectrum instrument derived from the Arab Qanūn; it is rarely absent in paintings of the fourteenth and fifteenth centuries where musical instruments are represented. The same instrument, increased in the weight of stringing to resist the impact of hammers, is the familiar dulcimer, which, like the hurdy-gurdy and the bagpipe, has seen better days. What was once thought of the dulcimer is shown by the painting that adorns the one drawn in Plate XVII. It seems almost vexatious that we do not know who first adjusted a key-board to a psaltery, and thus constructed a spinet. It was not earlier than the fifteenth century, but the name of the meritorious inventor has not come down to us, or where he lived. It seems most likely from the earliest name, clavicymbalum, being Latin, that the instrument was first contrived in a monastery. But we have, fortunately, in Plate VI., in an upright Spinet or Clavicytherium, one of the earliest existing specimens of the kind. It is a question not yet decided whether this rare instrument is of South German or North Italian origin. The reason is given for the former attribution in the description accompanying the drawing. Yet the Mantegnesque feeling is so strong in the decoration of the interior that we pause before accepting the Swabian origin as conclusively settled.

Queen Elizabeth's Virginal (Plate VIII.), which has at last found a resting-place in the splendid collection of old musical instruments in South Kensington Museum, is not a virginal proper, but apparently an Italian spinet. It has been gloriously decorated, and it awakens an intense feeling of interest to reflect upon who may have played upon it and who may have stood by and heard the pleasing tones of an instrument once so much cared for. The Spinet was at that time beginning to gain upon the Lute. The power to perform part music with two hands, which the lute-player, having only one hand to stop with, could but imperfectly approach, was an endowment there was no gainsaying. We may see the contemporary prosperity of the great Venetian republic in the lutes, theorboes, and spinets that are now dispersed throughout Europe; and almost at the same time such instruments as the Ruckers Virginal (Plate XVIII.) and the Ruckers double Spinet (Plate XX.) bear witness for Antwerp as to the favour successful commerce has ever shown the Arts. The great English spinet-makers belong to the second half of the seventeenth century, and the first quarter of the eighteenth. Among them, Stephen Keene was in the foremost rank, and his work will still bear examination in the spinet drawn in Plate XXII. The eighteenth century was marked by a great advance in making the expressive Clavichord, which although perhaps the oldest key-board stringed instrument, had always had to give way before the louder and more graceful-looking spinet. Plate XXXII. displays the clavichord at its culmination, and the Chinese Lac decoration shows that, in this specimen at least, its intimate charm of tone, capable, as no other key-board instrument was, of the *vibrato*, was deemed worthy of an elaborate setting.

The latest improvements of which the Spinet genus was capable, including the Venetian Swell, are founded in the Double Harpsichord (Plate XXXIII.) made by Burkat Shudi (Burkhard Tschudi) and John Broadwood in 1773, for the Empress Maria Theresa. It is a question whether some musical instruments of special character should not be retained for use or be made again when that character cannot be expressed by any existing instrument. If this were done the Viola d'Amore, the Viola da Gamba, the Harpsichord, the Clavichord, and the old German flute, in the last instance with some concession to defective intonation, would find their places and be sometimes heard with pleasure.

With regard to the selection and drawing of the subjects represented in the following Plates, it may be mentioned that the present writer had the important advantage of a free use of the remarkable Loan Collection of Musical Instruments exhibited at the Royal Albert Hall, Kensington, in 1885. Extraordinary facilities for drawing the selected subject were obtained through his official connection with the Music Division of the Exhibition, and through the gracious permission of the respective owners of the instruments, including H.M. the Queen, H.R.H. the Prince of Wales, H.R.H. the Siamese Minister, and the Japanese Commission. He has also utilised some sketches of instruments selected and drawn by Mr. Robert Glen of Edinburgh, to whom belongs the credit of originating the idea of this publication.

The pictorial representation of the subjects was undertaken by Mr. William Gibb, and the plates in this volume have been successfully reproduced from his admirable drawings. The book gains, moreover, a special and unexpected value from the fact that no illustrated Catalogue Raisonné was compiled of the Music

Loan Collection of 1885, which combined the most beautiful and valuable Manuscripts, Books, Paintings, etc., as well as Musical Instruments, which were ever brought together. There were no funds available, nor was there time to permit of such a work being carried out before the Collection was dispersed. By those who deplore the loss of that opportunity, the illustrations of this work may be regarded as a valuable memento of that unrivalled Collection.

A.J.H.

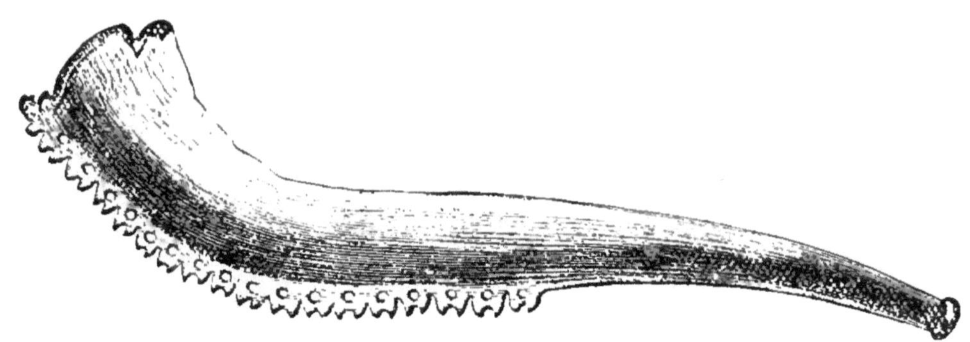

Jewish Shophar.

PLATE I.

BURGMOTE HORNS.

EAUTIFUL horns of hammered and embossed bronze belonging to the Corporations of Canterbury and Dover. The right-hand one is from Dover, where it was formerly used for the calling together of the Corporation at the order of the mayor. The minutes of the town proceedings were constantly headed "At a common Horn blowing" (comyne Horne Blowying). This practice continued until the year 1670, and is not yet entirely done away with, as it is still blown on the occasion of certain Municipal ceremonies. The motto on this horn is:—

JOHANNES DE · ALLEMAINE · ME · FECIT ·

preceded by the talismanic letters A·G·L·A, which stand for the Hebrew לְעוֹלָם אֲדֹנָי אַתָּה גִּבּוֹר and mean, "Thou art mighty for ever, O Lord!" The horn, which is 31¾ inches long, with a circumference at the larger end of 15½ inches, is of brass, and is deeply chased with a spiral scrollwork of foliage chiefly on a hatched ground. The inscription is on a band that starts four inches from the mouth and continues spirally. The maker's name is now nearly effaced, but the inscription shows that he was a German, and the date is assigned to the thirteenth century. A paper in the *Antiquary* (vol. 1. pp. 253-55), written by the late Llewellyn Jewitt, F.S.A., of which some use has here been made, states that there are on the obverse of the oldest Seal of Dover, said to have been made in 1305, two horn-blowers in the stern of a ship, each blowing a horn similar to this example.

The left-hand Burgmote Horn belongs to the Corporation of Canterbury, and records of its use for calling meetings of the Corporation are extant from 1376, down to the year 1835. The chord measurement of the arc of this Horn is 36 inches.

The antiquity of horns, whether natural or of metal, as instruments for sounding is well known. Their employment in some religious services points to customs that were already old when the oldest historical monuments we possess were raised. The Hebrew formulary upon the Dover horn reminds us of the Jewish Shophar, referred to particularly in the Introduction (page xiii)—a ram's horn, usually straightened and flattened, which is not only the solitary ancient musical instrument actually preserved in the Mosaic ritual, but is the oldest wind instrument known to be retained in present use in the world. It is still sounded by Jews on the New Year and on the Fast of the Day of Atonement.

In England, horns have been used amongst the various methods of transferring inheritances. They were adopted for instruments of conveyance either in Frank Almoigne, in Fee, or in Serjeantry, and from this cause have been often preserved.

Plate II.

PLATE II.

QUEEN MARY'S HARP.

HIS venerable instrument, the least impaired Gaelic Harp existing, is known as Queen Mary's Harp, and belongs to C. Durrant Steuart, Esq., of Dalguise, near Dunkeld. Of Gaelic Harps we can only reckon seven that may be dated earlier than the eighteenth century, the oldest being the Queen Mary and Lamont Harps, now in Edinburgh, and the harp named after Brian Boru (Boromha), preserved at Trinity College, Dublin; these three dating anterior, perhaps long anterior, to the fifteenth century. The Queen Mary and Brian Boru Harps are the two most nearly resembling one another. They are small, the Queen Mary Harp being only 31 inches high and 18 inches from back to front. They were played resting upon the left knee and against the left shoulder of the performer, whose left hand touched the upper strings. The comb is from 2½ to 3¼ inches high. It is inserted obliquely in the sound chest, and projects about 14 inches. The sound chest, in shape a truncated triangle hollowed out of the solid, is 5 inches wide at the top and 12 at the bottom, the depth being 4½ inches. The bow or forearm measures in a straight line 27½ inches, the chord of the arc of the inner curve being 23 inches. The front of it is expanded so as to form a convenient hold for the hand; it tapers slightly above and below, and ends both ways in boldly carved heads of animals of a symbolical character. The strings were of brass and twenty-nine in number, and were made to sound by the player's finger-nails, which were allowed to grow long for the purpose. The Queen Mary Harp has had another (the lowest) string attached later. This string measured 24 inches, the highest treble string 2½ inches; what compass the harp had it is now impossible to decide, but, following the tradition of Irish harpers, the accordance was based upon the old diatonic scale with the minor seventh, sometimes replaced by the major seventh. We learn by the lectures of the late Dr. Eugene O'Curry that the ancient Irish had three modes in their music, the "Crying," the "Laughing," and the "Sleeping." Whatever these tunings were, and probably the Highland Scotch had the same, their secret is locked up in the wood of the harps that once responded to them. In this, and frequent instances in these Plates, the instruments are not represented as strung. It is impossible to keep old instruments with that strain continually upon them, and to string them only to have them drawn would have been attended with many disadvantages.

The Queen Mary Harp has a history based upon the family tradition of its former owners, the Robertsons of Lude in Perthshire, but in passing through several mediums it has become unreliable. It was long believed to have been Mary Stuart's, and, according to the Lude tradition, it had golden and jewelled ornaments attached to the right upper circle of the bow including her portrait and the Royal Arms of Scotland, which were stolen about 1745. The historical inquiry containing the information respecting this Harp is by John Gunn, F.S.A.E., and was published in 1807, under the auspices of the Highland Society. A paper read before the Society of Antiquaries of Scotland by Mr. Charles D. Bell, F.S.A. Scot., and published in their *Proceedings* for 1880-81, from which I have made extracts, thoroughly sifts the facts that can be deduced from it, and which may be thus accepted:—Queen Mary of Lorraine, the mother of Mary Queen of Scots, gave this harp to Beatrix Gardyn of Banchory, Aberdeenshire. Beatrix Gardyn was married to Finla Mór, and from this marriage the family of Farquharson of Invercauld, in Braemar, is descended. Finla Mór was killed at the battle of Pinkie in A.D. 1547. John Robertson, the eleventh in succession to Lude, married Margaret Farquharson, the only daughter of the then Laird of Invercauld. He was fifty-six years in possession of Lude, and died in A.D. 1730. The last performer on this ancient harp was his great-grandson, General Robertson, who lent both the Lude harps for examination by the Highland Society in 1805. It appears to have been General Robertson's belief that this harp was acquired for Lude by the marriage of John, the eleventh Laird, with a direct descendant of Beatrix Gardyn, but, following Burke's genealogy of the family, it would appear that it came to Lude with Beatrix Gardyn herself, on her marriage with John, seventh Laird. The Robertsons of Lude are now, in the direct line, extinct, but the family of Gardyn is represented by Francis Garden-Campbell, Esq., of Troup and Glenlyon.

Queen Mary's and the Lamont Harps are on loan (1887) in the Museum of the Scottish Society of Antiquaries, Edinburgh, and it may be mentioned that when exhibited in the Music Loan Collection, South Kensington, the former was insured for £1500 and the latter for £1000.

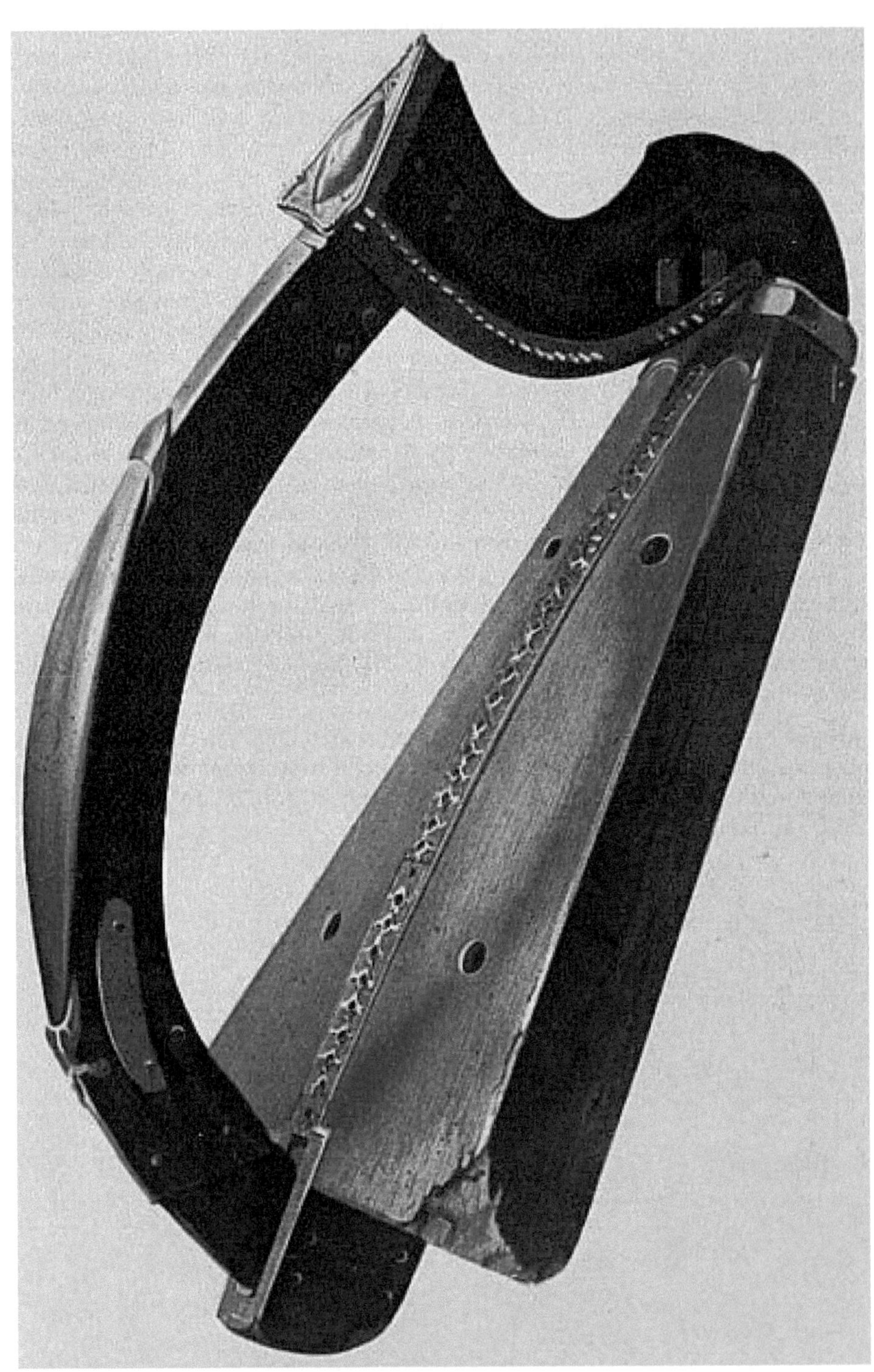

Plate III.

PLATE III.

THE LAMONT HARP.

THE Highland Harp, known as the Clarsach Lumanach, or Lamont Harp, belongs to the owner of the Queen Mary Harp, C. Durrant Steuart, Esq., of Dalguise, Perthshire. Both harps were sent to Edinburgh in 1805 by General Robertson of Lude, who owned them at that time, at the request of the Highland Society, and a book was published in 1807 under the patronage of the Society, entitled *An Historical Enquiry respecting the Performance on the Harp in the Highlands of Scotland from the earliest times until it was discontinued about the year 1734*, by John Gunn, F.A.S.E., in which they were described, and a version of the family tradition of Lude given, compiled from letters written by General Robertson, now unfortunately not forthcoming. Although Mr. Gunn's story of the Queen Mary Harp is coloured in order to attach the gift of it to Mary Queen of Scots, that of the Lamont Harp appears to be according to the simple statement of the original narrator, and may be thus epitomised from a paper published in the *Proceedings of the Society of Antiquaries of Scotland*, 1880-81, by Mr. C.D. Bell, F.S.A. Scot.: "The family tradition of Lude alleges that for several centuries past the larger of these harps has been known as the Clarsach Lumanach or Lamont Harp, and that it was brought from Argyllshire by a daughter of the Lamont family on her marriage with Robertson of Lude in 1464. It is said to be the older of the two. If the probably quiet place in the house of Lude be considered, and that it was likely to be valued and cared for there, also that the repairs appear to be of very old date, then the Clarsach Lumanach may have already, before 1464, been an old broken and mended instrument with a pre-traditional story we can never hope to hear." From Burke's *Landed Gentry*, "Lineage of the Robertsons of Lude," we learn that Charles, fifth Laird of Lude, married Lilias, daughter of Sir John Lamont of Lamont, chief of that clan, and that "it was with this lady, Lilias Lamont, there came one of those very curious old harps which have been in the family for several centuries."

The drawing shows the harp as it is, and may have been for centuries, but Mr. M'Intyre North, in his *Book of the Club of True Highlanders*, London, 1880, proposes, by the substitution of a longer bow or forearm, to bring this harp to the lines of the Queen Mary Harp and that of Brian Boru. It is sufficient here to observe that the present bow agrees in measurement with that of the Queen Mary and Brian Boru Harps, and is certainly very old. Against its originality is the fact that the Lamont Harp appears to have always had thirty-two strings, and for the three extra treble strings a longer bow ought to have been required.

The extreme length of the Lamont Harp is 38 inches, and the extreme width 18½ inches. The sound chest, as with other ancient harps, is hollowed out of one piece of wood, but the back has been in this instrument renewed, although probably a long time ago. The sound chest is 30 inches long, 4 inches in breadth at the top, and 17 at the bottom. The comb projects 15½ inches. The broken parts of the bow are held together by iron clamps.

As to the musical effect of a Gaelic or Irish harp when well played, the impression of such a performance recorded by Evelyn in his Diary is worth quoting. He says: "Came to see me my old acquaintance and the most incomparable player on the Irish harp, Mr. Clarke, after his travells. He was an excellent musitian, a discreete gentleman, borne in Devonshire (as I remember). Such musiq before or since did I never heare, that instrument being neglected for its extraordinary difficulty; but in my judgment it is far superior to the Lute itselfe, or whatever speakes with strings." Elsewhere he speaks of a Mr. Clark (probably the same performer) as being from Northumberland, and says of the instrument, "Pity 'tis that it is not more in use; but indeede to play well takes up the whole man, as Mr. Clark has assur'd me, who, tho' a gent of quality and parts, was yet brought up to that instrument from 5 yeares old, as I remember he told me."

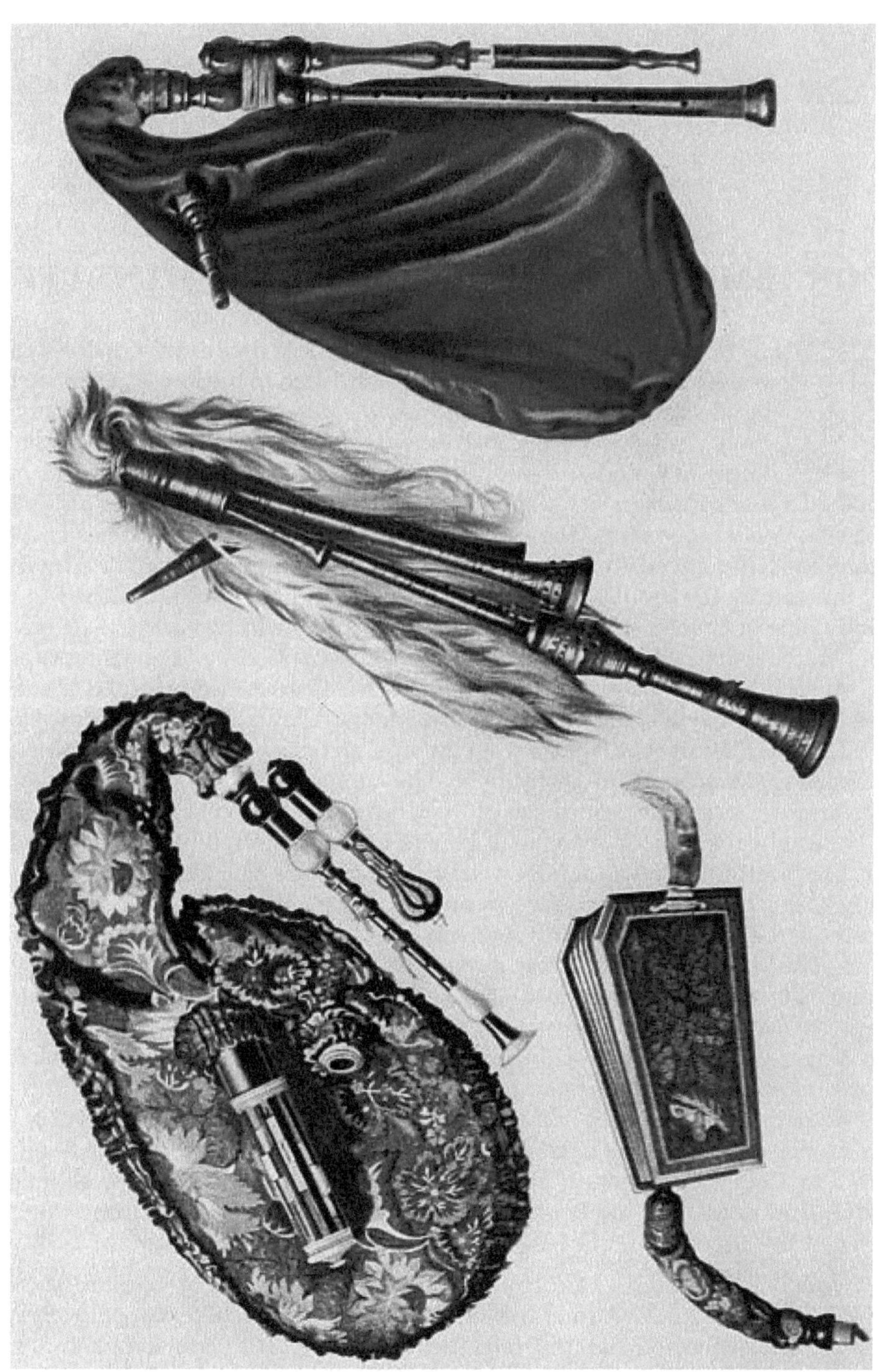

Plate IV.

PLATE IV.

CORNEMUSE, CALABRIAN BAGPIPE, MUSETTE.

THE Bagpipe (Cornemuse and Musette) and the hurdy-gurdy (Vielle) were, after the thirteenth century, banished to the lower orders, to the blind and to the wandering mendicant class. But polite society in France resumed these instruments again in the modern Arcadia of Louis XIV. and XV.—not the Cornemuse, it is true, for that has ever remained a rustic instrument, as may be observed in the glowing pages of George Sand's *Les Maîtres Sonneurs*. The Cornemuse, as formerly used in France and the Netherlands, is derived from the Roman *tibia utricularis,* and is provided with a bag, inflated by the mouth of the player, while a double reed is attached to the melody pipe or chanter. In recent times it is furnished with two drones—le grand, et le petit bourdon, which are made to sound also by reeds, and an octave apart. The Musette, which has practically displaced the Cornemuse in use, is a softer, sweeter instrument, with a double reed to a very narrow cylindrical pipe, the effect of which is to make it sound like a stopped pipe, an octave lower. This accounts for the short appearance of the instrument. The drones, as it will be seen, are on a more artificial principle than those of the Cornemuse. Another difference is that the bag is always inflated by a small pair of bellows worked by the player's left arm. The Northumbrian and modern Irish bagpipes are also inflated by means of bellows, and have taken the place in northern England and Ireland of the large bagpipe inflated with the mouth which is now regarded as distinctly Highland Scotch. The Musette in the drawing is made of ebony and ivory with keys of silver, and has a bag adorned with needlework. The small bellows are made of walnut inlaid with marqueterie. The melody pipe (le grand chalumeau) is bored with eight finger-holes, and fitted with seven keys for the chromatic notes. To the left of the melody pipe or chanter there is a small flask-shaped pipe furnished with six keys (le petit chalumeau) containing the additional compass upwards. There are four drones contrived in a barrel pierced with thirteen bores in juxtaposition, of from 5 to 35 inches in length. The barrel is furnished with five stops sliding in grooves and regulating the length of the apertures for tuning the drones. Bach's musettes, the alternatives to his gavottes, always imply a drone bass.

It will be observed the Cornemuse here drawn has a chanter and drone fixed parallel in one stock. The former has eight finger-holes, and, like that of the Scotch bagpipe, has a vent-hole not fingered. The bag covered with crimson plush is furnished with a short mouthpiece near the neck for the purpose of inflation.

The Calabrian Bagpipe or Zampogna is a rudely carved instrument of the eighteenth century. It has four drones attached to one stock, hanging downwards from the end of the bag: two of them are furnished with finger-holes. The reeds are double like those of the oboe and bassoon. The bag is large; it is inflated by the mouth and pressed by the left arm against the chest of the performer. The Zampogna is chiefly used as an accompaniment to a small reed melody pipe called by the same name, and played by another performer. The quality of the tone produced is not unpleasing. It has five holes only, and consequently the seventh of the scale is absent, but this can be easily got by octaving the open note of the pipe and covering part of the lower opening of the chanter with the little finger.

The Musette, Zampogna, and Cornemuse here shown are from specimens belonging to Messrs. J. & R. Glen, Edinburgh.

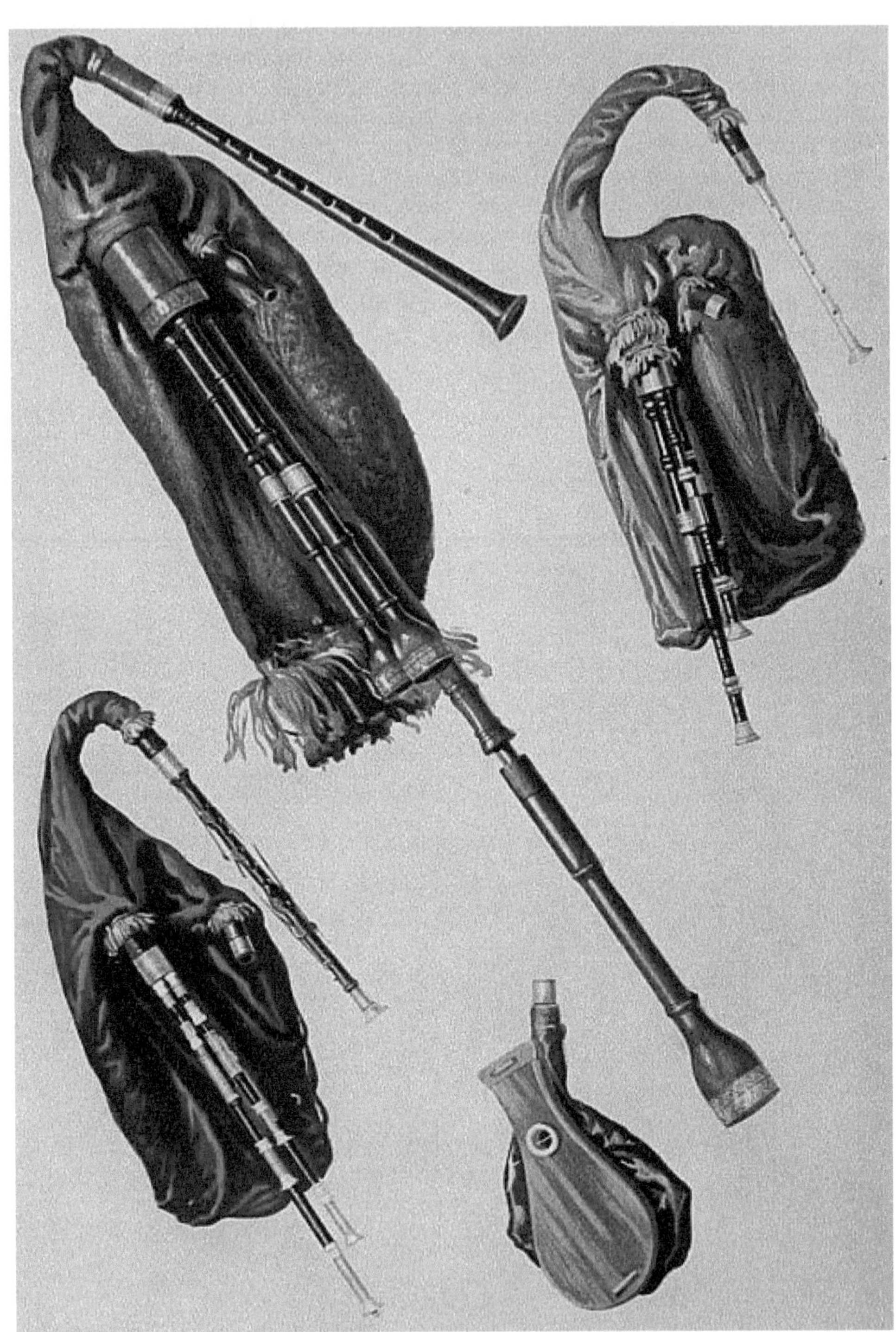

Plate V.

PLATE V.

BAGPIPES.

IN continuation of the Bagpipes, this Plate shows, in the instrument with a crimson bag, the modern Northumbrian Bagpipe. The four drones, proceeding from one stock, are mounted with brass and ivory. The chanter, or melody pipe, has seven finger-holes in front and one behind; also, seven brass keys. As there is only one hole open at a time when the instrument is played, this manner of playing is called close fingering. The chanter and drones are furnished with stops at the ends. The instrument with a blue bag is the ancient Northumbrian bagpipe. It has three drones, mounted with silver and ivory, of different sizes; the longest being tuned an octave and the middle one a fourth lower than the shortest. The chanter is of ivory, with seven holes in front and one behind. The large bagpipe with a green bag is the Lowland Scotch. It is of boxwood, with three drones placed in one stock. The two shorter drones sound in unison, the long one an octave lower, the same as in the Highland Bagpipe. They are mounted with carved horn. The chanter has seven finger-holes and a vent-hole, also the same as in the Highland Bagpipe, with which the Lowland agrees in fingering and other particulars, except that it is inflated by bellows attached to the bag by a short blow-pipe, a peculiarity that it has in common with the other Bagpipes in this Plate. The bellows of the modern Northumbrian Bagpipe are also drawn.

The Bagpipe is, as Mr. Henri Lavoix has justly said in his *La Musique au Siècle de Saint Louis*, the organ reduced to its most simple expression. It is of great antiquity, and in the Middle Ages was generally popular in Europe. It was as well known in England as in Scotland, in France as in Italy and Germany. Shakspeare makes out Falstaff in Part I. of Henry IV. to be as melancholy as a lover's lute or the drone of a Lincolnshire Bagpipe. If we may judge by the peculiar scale of the Scotch Bagpipe, it would appear almost certain that the instrument, in its modern forms, has come from the East, and was most likely brought by the Crusaders. This would not of course apply to the ancient principle of a pipe and air reservoir, which is traced back to the Romans, but to the boring of the finger-holes of the chanter, the reed pipe by which the melody is played. By their position and size the intervals are so regulated that the thirds are neither major nor minor, but give a neutral or mean interval that is neither the one nor the other. This mean third, of a tone and three-quarters, has not been elsewhere observed in Europe, but in the East, in Syria and Egypt, and in other parts, it is of common occurrence, and gives a peculiar character to the music, not to be explained, but felt. An historical origin of the mean third is to be found in Mr. A.J. Ellis's paper "On the Musical Scales of Various Nations" (p. 498), published in the *Journal of the Society of Arts*, London, March, 1885. Modern Bagpipes that have keys are, of course, different.

As to the antiquity of existing Bagpipes, Messrs. Glen of Edinburgh own one, carved with the initials R. M[c].D., and the Hebridean galley, that bears the date of 1409. But this is not considered to be the oldest existing, as the M'Intyre pipe, belonging to N. Robertson M'Donald, Esq., of Kinlochmoidart, is reputed to have been played at Bannockburn. Possessing one drone only, it has the peculiarity of two vent-holes, instead of one, on each side of the chanter to accommodate a right or left handed player; in either case one hole is temporarily stopped. Messrs. Glen's pipe has two drones set in one stock. The name M'Intyre, by which Mr. Robertson M'Donald's pipe is distinguished, is derived from the hereditary pipers of the Chiefs of Menzies and Clanranald. Both these ancient Bagpipes are figured in Mr. M'Intyre North's *Book of the Club of True Highlanders*. The Bagpipes here drawn are from specimens belonging to Messrs. J. & R. Glen, Edinburgh.

Plate VI.

PLATE VI.

CLAVICYTHERIUM OR UPRIGHT SPINET.

HIS singularly interesting and rare key-board instrument, now the property of Mr. Donaldson, belonged to the collection of Count Correr of Venice. There is no maker's name or any date upon the instrument, which is of the kind named Clavicytherium by the earliest writer on musical instruments, Virdung (*Musica getutscht und auszgezogen*, Basle, 1511), who gives a drawing of one. It is in fact a spinet, set upright. The internal decoration, as old as the instrument itself, may be North Italian or South German, authorities differ, but a piece of paper pasted over a split in the inside of the wooden back, possibly by the maker, proves to be a fragment of a lease or agreement contracted at Ulm, which is in favour of the Swabian origin. The instrument can hardly be of later date than the first years of the sixteenth century, and is probably the oldest spinet or key-board stringed instrument existing. The earliest date that can be given for the introduction of the Spinet must be within the second half of the fifteenth century.

The key-board is of narrow compass—three octaves and a minor third—from the second E below, to the second G above, middle C, this note being the ledger-line C between the bass and treble clefs —an extent about the compass of the human voice, which long ruled that of key-board instruments. In Virdung's time their compass was being extended. It is, however, more than likely that the lowest E key was here tuned down to the still lower C, according to the so-called "short octave" arrangement, which altered the lowest E, F♯, and G♯, to make fourths below F, G, and A, instead of semitones, and thus get deep dominant basses for cadences. Examination of the plectra or "jacks" of this instrument shows they were furnished with little tongues of wire, and not quills or leather, as in later spinet instruments. It is in a painted pine case, the inside being also painted. An unusual feature of the interior is the Calvary below the narrow sound-board, in which the sound holes, judging by the ornament that remains in one, have been Flamboyant windows. There must also have originally been figures, perhaps the Transfiguration or the Crucifixion, but there is no trace of them left. The treatment of the landscape, without other evidence, nearly determines the epoch when the instrument was made.

The stand and the paintings on the door, one of which represents a figure holding a mirror and a serpent, are of later date.

The dimensions of this truly remarkable spinet are—height of instrument, 4 feet 10½ inches, and extreme width, 2 feet 3 inches—the key-board being 2 feet wide. The depth of the case at base, 11 inches, diminishes in ascending to 5⅝ inches. The table upon which it stands is 2 feet high and 2 feet 11 inches wide.

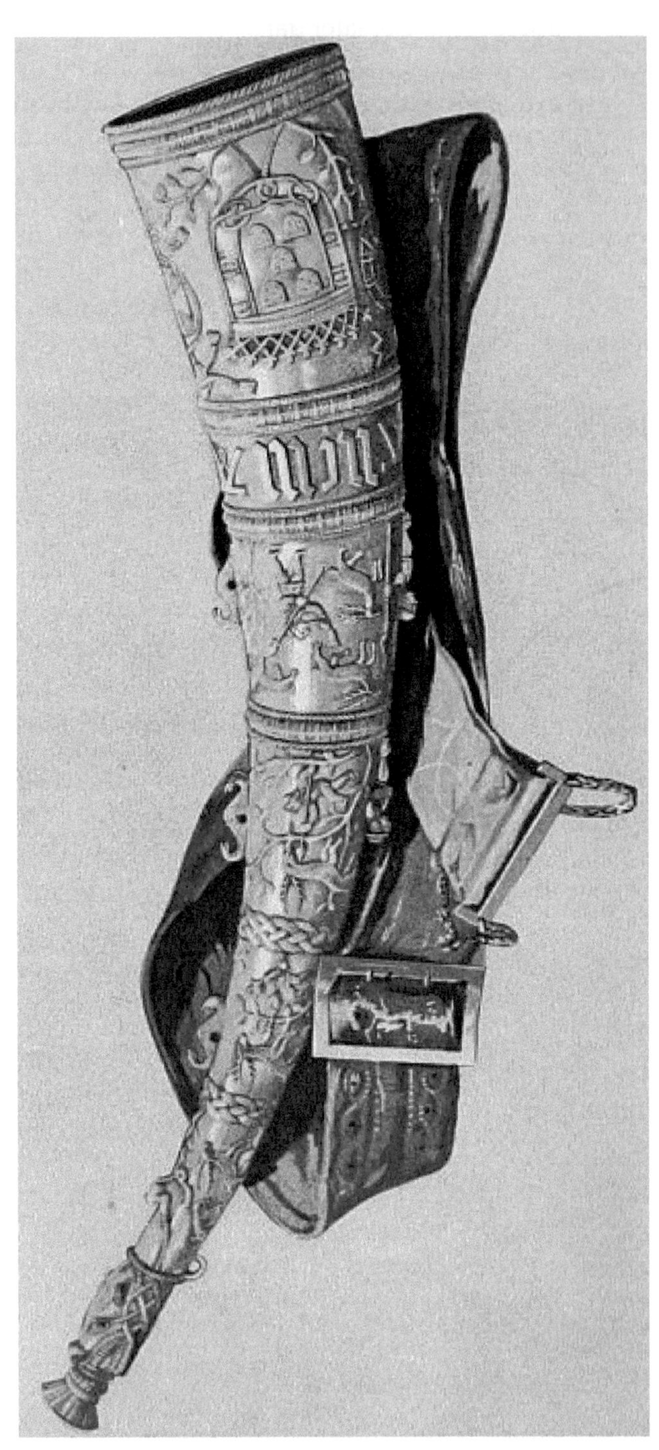

Plate VII.

PLATE VII.

OLIPHANT.

AN ivory Hunting Horn belonging to Earl Spencer, called Oliphant because it is of ivory, and bearing in the ornament the arms and badges of Ferdinand and Isabella of Portugal, may be regarded as belonging to the first half of the sixteenth century, the strap and buckle being evidently an addition of later date. The beautiful carving, so conspicuous in this horn, is supposed to have been executed by negroes of the West Coast of Africa, who carved ivory for the Portuguese; the arms of Portugal, with the supporters, two angels, holding the shield upside down, often appearing on their work.

Philip II. of Spain married Mary, daughter of the King of Portugal, in 1543. She died in 1545. The carving of the Horn was probably completed within that interval, and when Philip came to England to marry Mary Tudor, he may have brought the horn with him.

Besides the uses named under Burgmote Horns (Plate I.) horns were blown to give alarm in circumstances of danger, to announce the arrival of visitors of distinction, and, as Mr. M'Intyre North informs us respecting the horn in Drummond Castle, for summoning the household and guests to dinner. But horns were not restricted to winding, there were also drinking and powder horns, often beautifully adorned.

The extreme length of this Horn, measuring along the outside of the curve and including the mouthpiece, is 28¼ inches. The greatest circumference is 11½ and the least 2¾ inches.

Plate VIII.

PLATE VIII.

QUEEN ELIZABETH'S VIRGINAL.

THIS beautiful Spinet is, in the drawing, placed upon a stand, which served for its support in the Tudor Historical Room appertaining to the Music Loan Collection of 1885. I believe this instrument to be Italian, not Flemish or English, and Italian spinets had no stands or legs, but when required for use were withdrawn from an outer case, as this one would be, and placed upon a table, or some other convenient position. They were even taken in Gondolas, as Evelyn records, for pleasure and the performance of serenades.

We may assume 1570 to be approximately the date of this instrument. The green and gold decoration, including a border of gold two and a half inches broad round the inside of the top, is of later date, perhaps by nearly one hundred years. An indistinct number on the back of the case, inside, appears to be 1660. The Royal Arms of Elizabeth are emblazoned on one end to the left of the key-board; to the right a dove is seen rising crowned. The dove holds in its right foot a sceptre; beneath it is an oak tree. This decoration, whether original in 1660 or the copy of a former one, goes far to support the claim for this Spinet having been Queen Elizabeth's. Her musical taste, inherited from Elizabeth of York, and skill as a performer upon the spinet, need no more than a passing reference.

I characterize the instrument as a spinet because a true virginal is a parallelogram, not a trapeze-shaped instrument. The attribution of virginal is, however, not incorrect as a generic term; for all key-board stringed instruments with jacks were known in England as virginals from the Tudor epoch to that of the Commonwealth.

There are in this instrument fifty quilled jacks (plectra). The natural keys, thirty in number, are of ebony with gold arcaded fronts, and the compass is of four octaves and apparently a semitone, from B to C. But the lowest natural key was tuned G when the instrument was in use. The semitone keys, twenty in number, begin apparently as C♯, but this was tuned A to continue the "short octave" arrangement. They are very elaborate, being inlaid with silver, ivory, and different woods, each consisting, it is said, of about two hundred and fifty pieces. The painting of the case of the instrument is done upon gold with carmine and ultramarine, the metal ornaments being minutely engraved. The outer case is of cedar, covered with crimson Genoa velvet, and lined inside with yellow tabby silk. There are three gilt locks, finely engraved. The entire case is five feet long, sixteen inches wide, and seven inches deep. Queen Elizabeth's Virginal was bought, at Lord Spencer Chichester's sale at Fisherwick in 1803, by Mr. Jonas Child, a painter at Dudley. The Rev. J.M. Gresley acquired it in 1840. It has since (1887) been obtained from the Rev. Nigel Gresley, for South Kensington Museum.

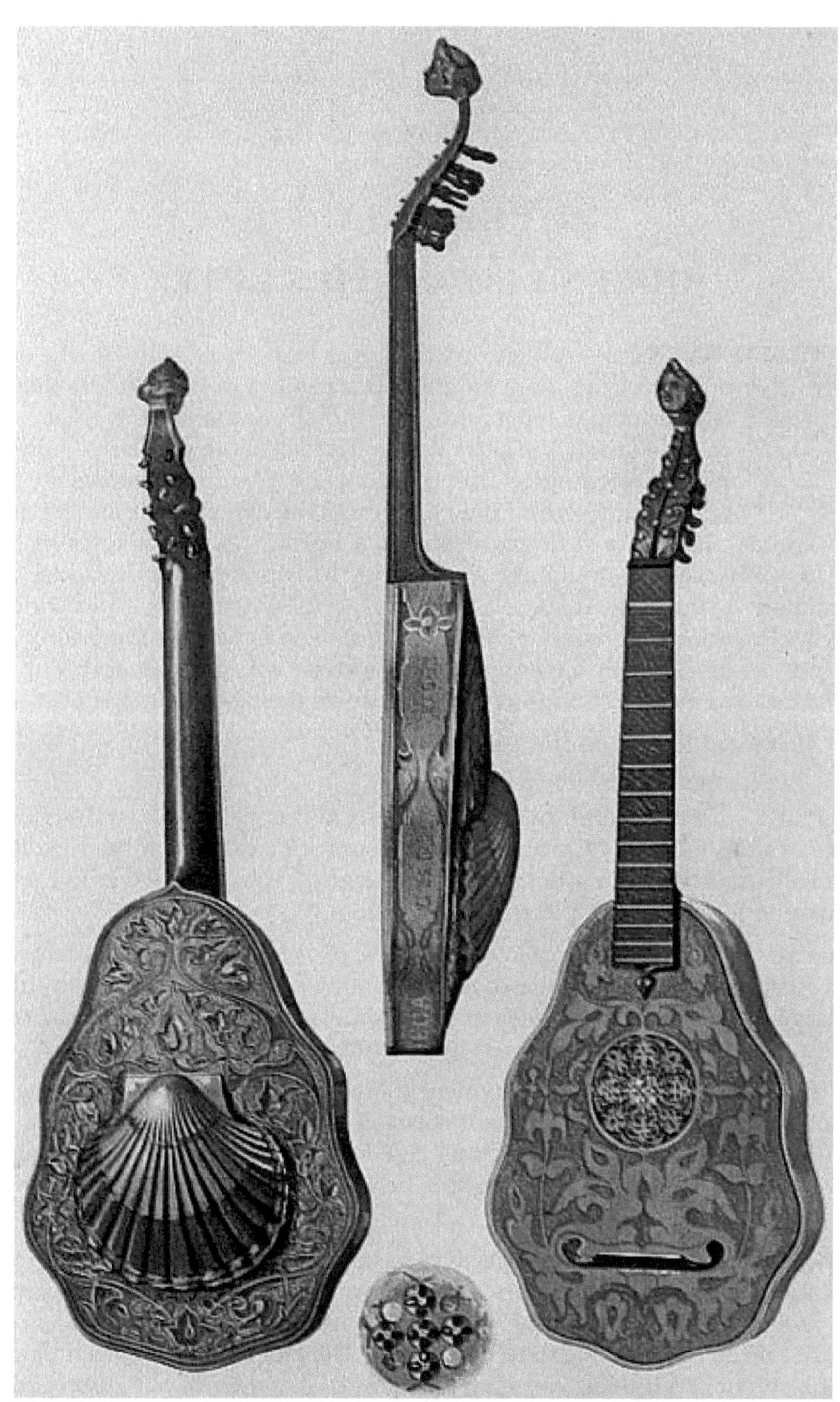

Plate IX.

PLATE IX.

QUEEN ELIZABETH'S LUTE.

STRINGED instruments with a finger-board, touched with the fingers or a plectrum, may be divided, as stated in the Introduction, into two principal types: the lute and the guitar, the former with a rounded back, the latter with a flat back. Both are derived from the East. According to this division, the beautiful instrument called Queen Elizabeth's Lute must resign the name of lute and be considered a Guitar. As a wire-strung instrument it belongs to that species of guitar known as Cither, and from the incurvations of the ribs, but that the bridge is not set obliquely, I should be disposed to specialize the instrument as a Pandore or Penorcon. Praetorius regarded the Pandore and its varieties, the Orpheoreon and Penorcon, as of English invention. This instrument, the property of Lord Tollemache, was made in London by John Rose, as the label bears witness:—

> Johannes Rosa, Londini fecit,
> In Bridwell, the 27th of July, 1580.

It is infinitely more graceful than any Pandore, and is perhaps best described by the maker's designation, "Cymbalum Decachordum," carved on the ribs. It had, as this name indicates, ten strings, which were of wire, to be tuned in five pairs of unisons, and played with a plectrum.

The carving is surpassingly lovely, and bears comparison with contemporary Italian work. The jewelled centre of the rose in the sound-hole is so beautiful that an enlarged drawing of it has been made to show it to advantage. The shell at the back is a characteristic feature deserving attention.

The extreme length of this instrument is 2 feet 11 inches. The length of the body is 1 foot 4 inches. The extreme breadth, beneath the rose and near the string-holder, is 12 inches. The breadth, measuring across the centre of the rose, is 10 inches. The depth of the ribs varies from 1½ to 3 inches, the greatest depth being near the finger-board.

The traditions that attach themselves to instruments of this character require to be carefully tested. Queen Mary's Harp, for instance, could not have been the gift to Beatrix Gardyn from Mary Stuart of Scots, although her portrait and coat of arms are said to have, at one time, adorned it. The attribution to Queen Elizabeth also of a spinet or virginal rests entirely upon such evidence as can be gathered from the instrument itself. This so-called lute has no doubt the support of a family tradition, and the story is thus told in Burke's *Peerage* ("Lineage of the Dysart

Family," 1884): "Sir Lionel Tollemache, of Helmingham, high sheriff of Norfolk and Suffolk in 1567. In 1561 Queen Elizabeth honoured Helmingham with her presence, and remained there from the 14th to the 18th of August inclusive, being most hospitably and sumptuously entertained. During Her Majesty's visit she stood sponsor to Sir Lionel's son, and presented the child's mother with her lute, which is still preserved at Helmingham Hall, county Suffolk, the seat of Lord Tollemache of Helmingham." Unfortunately the dates do not fit. John Rose's Lute, made in 1580, although it might possibly have belonged to Queen Elizabeth, could not have been the lute given in 1561. It is the tradition, however, that may have gone astray, and a fault in it does not do away entirely with a plausible attribution.

Plate X.

PLATE X.

THE RIZZIO GUITAR.

THIS beautiful Guitar of tortoiseshell, combined with ivory, mother-o'-pearl, and ebony (the property of Mr. George Donaldson, London), has ten pegs representing fleur-de-lys, and the ornament round the rose is formed with the same emblematic flower. To this, no doubt, it owes its romantic reputation of having belonged to David Rizzio. The apparent age of the Guitar would agree with a supposed gift of it from Mary Stuart to Rizzio, and the fleur-de-lys might connect it with the French or Scotch Royal Families; but this slender suggestion of the fleur-de-lys, to which the guitar owes its special interest, unsupported by other evidence, is scarcely sufficient to uphold the fascinating attribution. Mr. Donaldson, however, informs me that this instrument was bought in Scotland, nearly forty years ago, from an old family that had possessed it for generations with this tradition of its former ownership.

This Guitar had ten strings, forming five notes, in pairs of unisons, instead of six single strings, as in the modern guitar, giving six notes. It is the lowest note E that is here wanting. The instrument is 3 feet 1 inch in extreme length; the body being 18¾ inches in length, and 10 inches across. The ribs are 3¾ inches deep.

This Spanish guitar may have first come to England in the reign of Henry VIII., as there is occasional mention, at that time, of the Spanish viol, a bowed instrument which may have been accompanied by the true Spanish guitar. There is no doubt, however, about the Spanish guitar having been here in the reign of Elizabeth, and it might have been brought by attendants of Philip II. when he married Mary Tudor. In the latter half of the sixteenth century it was already known, valued, and highly decorated in Venice; and it was also known in France, so that, as an instrument, it would not be strange to Mary Stuart, or Rizzio either. The lute, however, was the most in vogue at that time, excepting perhaps in Spain. The character of the design of this so-called Rizzio guitar is undoubtedly Moorish.

Plate XI.

PLATE XI.

POSITIVE ORGAN.

CHAMBER Organ formerly in the Tolbecque Collection, and belonging to the epoch of Louis XIII. The Positive Organ, as the name implies, was intended to remain in a fixed place, while the smaller portable organ (orgue portatif) was made to be carried about. The disposition of the pipes was usually the same in both organs,—what may be called the natural order,—ascending from the longest pipe in the bass to the shortest in the treble, but some positive organs had the pipes arranged in a circular disposition, perhaps for a more equal distribution of the weight upon what is known as the sound-board. The instrument admits of more than one register. There are authentic representations of positives in several old pictures, one of the best known being that in the St. Cecilia panel, by Hubert Van Eyck, in the famous altar-piece of the Adoration of the Lamb at Ghent. The original St. Cecilia panel, now at Berlin, was not painted later than 1426, but the panel at Ghent is a good copy. Another St. Cecilia panel (date about 1484), with a positive organ, by an unknown painter, is not of such universal fame, but is nevertheless of very great merit. It is in the palace of Holyrood, Edinburgh, and is of equal value with the Van Eyck panel as a faithful representation of the instrument, and of the chromatic arrangement of the keys, thus early introduced.

The Positive Organ drawn in this volume has been intended for chamber, not choir, use. It has three registers, and the drawstops which control them project at the right-hand side of the case the same as in the old Flemish harpsichords. The principal register, that of the show pipes of gilt tin, is called the Montre; and the compass of it is from the E below, to the third C above, middle C—three octaves and a sixth. The second register, also of tin, is an octave higher in pitch, but extends only from the first E below, to the second C above, middle C; the remainder of the key-board compass is borrowed from the Montre. The third register is the Bourdon—wooden pipes stopped at the upper ends, an octave lower in pitch than the Montre. The Bourdon extends in compass from E an octave and sixth below, to the second C above, middle C. The three registers in this instrument are consequently at octave distances, but Praetorius (1619) describes an old positive in which the registers were in the relation of the fifth and octave to the lowest!—a combination the modern musical ear rejects. The boxwood natural keys with gilded paper fronts, as seen in this specimen, were common to the earliest known keyboard instruments. The dimensions of this Positive Organ, including the stand, are—height, 6 feet 4 inches; width, 2 feet 6 inches; and depth, 1 foot 4 inches.

The paintings inside the doors are, to the left, St. Cecilia playing upon a positive organ, while three angels sing and a fourth blows the bellows; to the right, a warrior crowned with laurel is in the attitude of listening; outside the doors there are panels with paintings of a woman playing on an instrument of the viol kind, and another playing a flute. There is a crowing cock upon the apex of the cornice. This Positive Organ is the property of the Conservatoire Royal, Brussels.

Plate XII.

PLATE XII.

REGAL.

HE Regal here drawn is the prototype of the modern harmonium, but with "beating" not "free" reeds. The beating reed is usually employed in the organ, and it derives its appellation from the reeds touching the sides of their frames. The beating reed was introduced in the fifteenth century, but whether in the simple regal first, or as part of an organ, is not known. In England, the word "regal" has been also used to denote a portable organ, as is shown by Sir John Hawkins's suggestion that the stage direction to the players' scene in Hamlet, "Enter a duke and a duchess with regal coronets," should be "with regals and cornets." The oldest German authorities, as Virdung (1511) and Praetorius (1619), separate them and describe the regal as a reed instrument with key-board exactly like this one, a kind of positive and not a portable organ. This Regal, which was in the Tolbecque Collection, is attributed in date to the end of the sixteenth century. It came from the Abbey of Freuenfeld in Switzerland, and now belongs to the Brussels Conservatoire. Mr. Victor Mahillon, the curator of the museum of that institution, records another fine specimen of this very rare instrument in the possession of the Community of Lady Canonesses of the order of St. Augustine, at Brussels, to which body it was presented, by the founder of the Order, in 1625. The regal is said to have been much used in convents to accompany the singing of the nuns. The Belgian Government kindly allowed a selection of the Conservatoire instruments, of which the Regal here drawn was one, to be played in the Historic Concerts given in July 1885, in the Music Room of the Inventions Exhibition. This instrument, when on its stand, measures 2 feet 8 inches in height, the width is the same, and the length is 4 feet 2 inches. The case is of finely-carved walnut. The compass of the key-board is from the second E below, to the second A above, middle C—about the extent of the human voice, and the frequent compass of old organs.

The word "regal" has been derived from the inventor having made a present of the first one to a king, or to kings having had in their establishments special regal-makers. Rigabello, a now unknown instrument which is said to have preceded the organ in Venice, is also quoted as the origin of the name. I have elsewhere (*Encyclopædia Britannica*, article Pianoforte) suggested that "regal" may have come from "regula," a rule, the idea of gradation being inherent in a key-board. The wooden harmonicon, when made to play by a key-board, was at one time called regal (régale en bois).

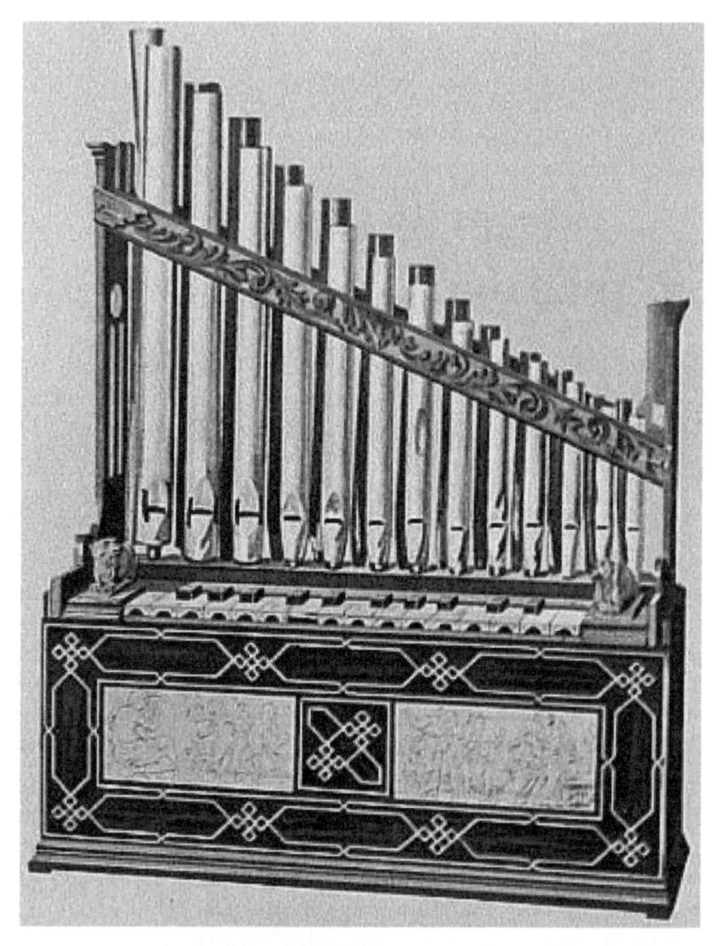

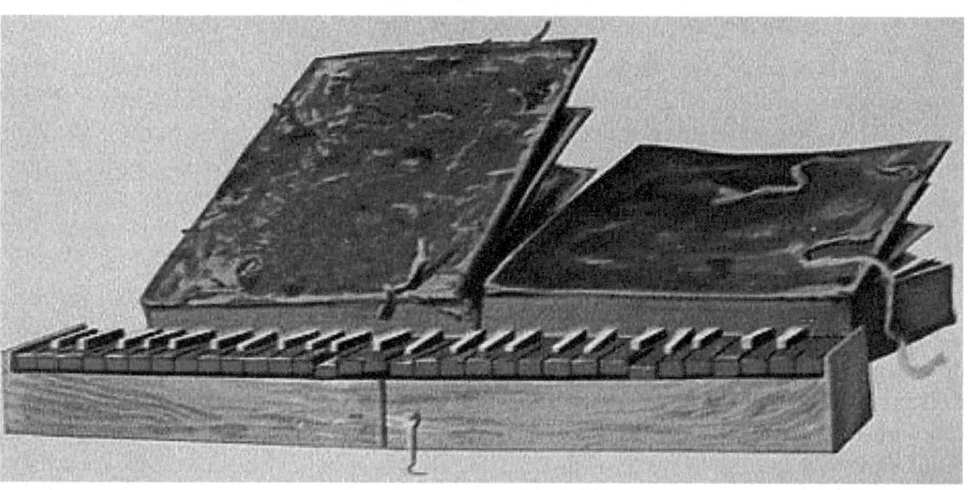

Plate XIII.

PLATE XIII.

PORTABLE ORGAN AND BIBLE REGAL.

HE Portable Organ (orgue portatif, also nimfali) was a processional instrument slung by a strap over the player's shoulder, so as to allow the bellows at the back of the instrument to be worked by the player's left hand, while the keys were touched with the fingers of the right hand. From the high pitch of the pipes, the limited number of keys, and one hand only being used for touching them, it is possible that only one voice, or part, was played. The same remarks may be made of the early large organs, except that, with them, each key made several pipes of various lengths speak at the same time, so as to give the octave, twelfth, and super-octave, and still higher accordant intervals,—in point of fact, the large organ was, with the exception of the front pipes, a large mixture stop. The positive and portable organs were smaller editions of the principal or front pipe part of the large organ. From Orcagna and Fra Angelico, in the fourteenth century, to D.G. Rossetti and E. Burne Jones, in the nineteenth, the portable organ has been a favourite musical instrument for delineation by the painter of religious subjects, and from the fourteenth to the seventeenth centuries no musical instrument was more in favour in religious establishments. Notwithstanding this fact, I know of only two as now existing, and they are both of late date, being of the seventeenth century. The one, here drawn, belongs to the Museum of the Brussels Conservatoire, while the other, belonging to His Grace the Duke of Athole, is preserved at Blair Athole in Scotland.

The Brussels Portable Organ has twenty-six metal pipes arranged in two rows, and has as many keys, in a compass extending from the first E to the third F above middle C. On the case are engravings upon wood and ivory, representing a youth playing upon a harp while three boys dance, and a woman playing upon a portable organ while a girl and two boys sing. A woodcut of the harp-player is on the title-page of this volume. There is a conventional lion on each key-block. The dimensions are—height, 2 feet 6 inches; width, 2 feet; and depth, 8 inches.

The Bible Regal, drawn in the same Plate, is of the same kind as the beating reed Regal. The pipes which enclose the reeds are so cut down as to practically do little more than cover them. The instrument is so constructed that it can be folded up, and, when closed, looks like a book—whence the name Bible Regal. The key-board, hinged in the middle, is extended for performance. In the instrument drawn it is of four octaves and a fourth compass. The bellows are found by reversing the book cover. The Bible Regal is said to have been invented about the middle of the sixteenth century, by George Voll, an organ-builder of Nuremberg.

It is extremely rare; I only know of two, one belonging to Mr. Wyndham Portal of Malshanger, Basingstoke, and this instrument, the property of Mrs. Frederick Pagden and her sister Miss Ferrari.

Plate XIV.

PLATE XIV.

CETERA.

HE instrument, in Italian "Cetera," is in French called "Cistre," and in English "Cither," sometimes English Guitar. It belongs to the guitar kind because it has a flat back, but all cithers are strung with wire, and the sounds are elicited, like those of the lute-shaped mandoline, by means of a plectrum. This exquisitely beautiful instrument of the early sixteenth century is attributed to the Brescian School. Formerly the property of the Biblioteca Estense at Modena, it has since been acquired by Mr. George Donaldson, London. It will be observed in the drawing that a carving of a woman's head surmounts the peg-box and resolves itself into a lizard, which serves as a handle wherewith to hold the instrument. A mermaid is seen below the finger-board, and there are two in the carving of the back. The ribs are also carved. To show this exquisite carving upon a larger scale enlargements are given of the finger-board mermaid and the rose in the sound-hole. The extreme length of the instrument is 3 feet; and that of the body measured to the neck, 19½ inches; the number of strings is thirteen. Praetorius gives the tuning of such an instrument as follows: the highest being the single melody string.

This Cetera should be compared with that of Mr. Alard in Plate XXVIII.—an instrument made by the famous violin-maker, Antonio Stradivari.

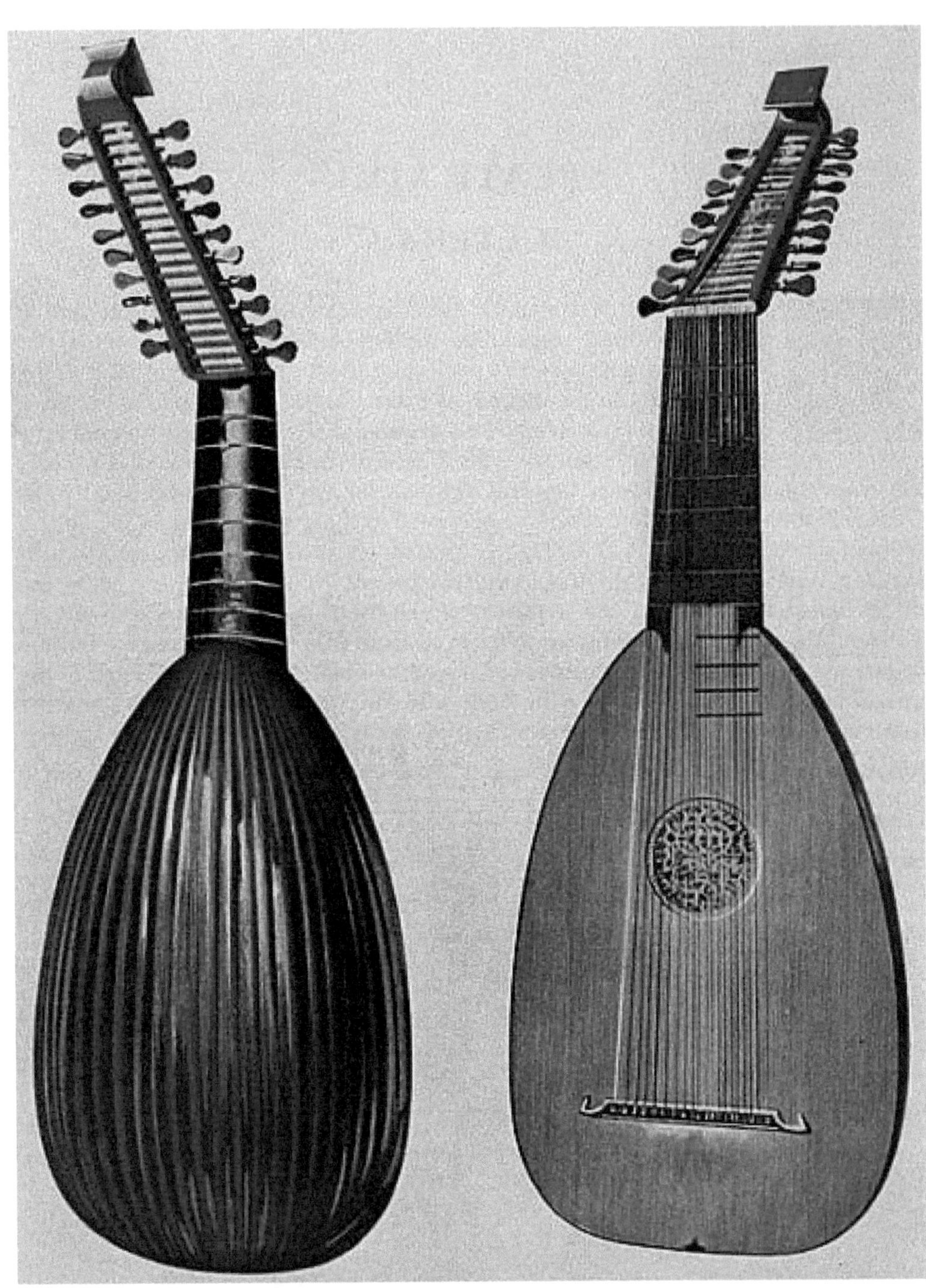

Plate XV.

PLATE XV.

LUTE.

A FINE old Italian Lute, with the label "1600, In Padova Vvendelio Venere." It is not only rare, but a special interest is attached to it from its having been the favourite musical instrument of the late Carl Engel. When he disposed of his collection he reserved this instrument for his own use, and probably his last performance upon it was Handel's "Lascia ch'io pianga," which he played to the present writer, who now owns the instrument.

It is a large lute, being 42 inches in length. The greatest width of the body is 14½ inches, with an extreme depth of 8 inches. The body is 21 inches from the base to the shoulders; from thence to the nut is 10¾ inches, and it is 13½ inches from the nut to the extremity of the head, the angle of the peg-box being obtuse. The mean width of the finger-board is 4 inches. It is furnished with twenty strings, which are divided into six pairs of unisons, and eight single strings for basses. Engel tuned it in the D minor tuning, an accordance introduced according to Herr Oscar Fleischer in the first half of the seventeenth century, by the great French lutenist, Denis Gaultier. This accordance ultimately prevailed not only in France and England but in Germany; the same writer informs us that Joseph Haydn used it. This lute, when so tuned, is thus arranged—

but the old Lute tuning was, in chamber pitch—

Mersenne (*Harmonie Universelle,* Paris, 1636) places this finger-board scale a tone higher, with the Chanterelle on A. This change really infers the use of a lower pitch. By Gaultier's tuning the strain is taken off the highest note—a relief of much importance, when the high chamber pitch then customary, nearly a whole tone above the normal French pitch, is considered. By the twelve frets upon the finger-board for the highest notes, the melody strings could be raised chromatically one octave, thus making the extreme compass of the instrument four octaves and a note, from the third F below, to the second G above, middle C. Before the year 1600 the lute was played, as the old tablatures or lute notations show us, in single notes with occasional chords, a practice derived from lute-playing frequently found in modern pianoforte music. There were attempts at counterpoint, but these were limited, owing to one hand only being available for stopping. Certain graces were used, especially the *vibrato,* but there is reason to believe they were used for some time by the players before the composers thought fit to indicate them. With the growing favour for simple chords, which were developed into the Continuo or Thorough Bass accompaniment, the bass strings—diapasons, as they were called—were added beneath the finger-board accordance to be tuned for basses as the player required. At last they were attached by the contrivance of a double neck to a higher peg-box, by which the Lute became a Theorbo. Both varieties were superseded early in the eighteenth century by the guitar, which was easier to play, and the immensely popular spinet, which permitted the performance of a complete counterpoint, by the freedom it gave to use both hands upon the key-board. A reflection might here be made on the masterly way in which contemporary painters drew hands and lutes. I need only name those masters of the Dutch school, Frans Hals, Jan Steen, and Terburg, especially Steen, whose truthful precision compels admiration. Of another school, there is a lute-player drawn by Albrecht Dürer, that is a miracle of skill and accuracy of observation.

A considerable literature of the lute exists belonging to the sixteenth, seventeenth, and eighteenth centuries. Thomas Mace (1676) writes very amusingly about it. He accounts Venice lutes as commonly good, but gives the highest place to Laux Maler of Bologna. Evelyn, in his Diary, also quotes Bologna as famous for lutes, especially those of the old masters, Mollen, Hans Frey, and Nicholas Sconvelt (*sic*), who were Germans. The first-named is probably intended for Maler. In Evelyn's time, lutes by these makers were fetching extraordinary prices. The most interesting modern works of information about the lute, as well as of contemporary music generally, are *La Musique aux Pays Bas*, Edmond Vander Straeten (Brussels, 1867-85), from a future volume of which a monograph has been published in anticipation, entitled *Jacques de Saint-Luc, Luthiste Athois du xviie siècle* (Mayence, 1887); *Musique et Musiciens au xviie siècle,* a publication of the "Société pour l'Histoire Musicale des Pays-Bas," edited by W.J.A. Jonckbloet and J.P.N. Land, and containing the musical correspondence of the astronomer Constantin Huygens (Leyden, 1882); and a monograph upon the famous Parisian lutenist, Denis Gaultier, by Oscar Fleischer, published in the *Vierteljahrschrift für Musikwissenschaft* for January and April 1886 (Leipsic, Breitkopf and Härtel). The first three-quarters of the seventeenth century was a period remarkable for a refined amateur cultivation of instrumental music. Shakspeare's appreciation of the lute, and his graceful tribute of admiration for the performance of his friend, the lutenist Dowland, are well known.

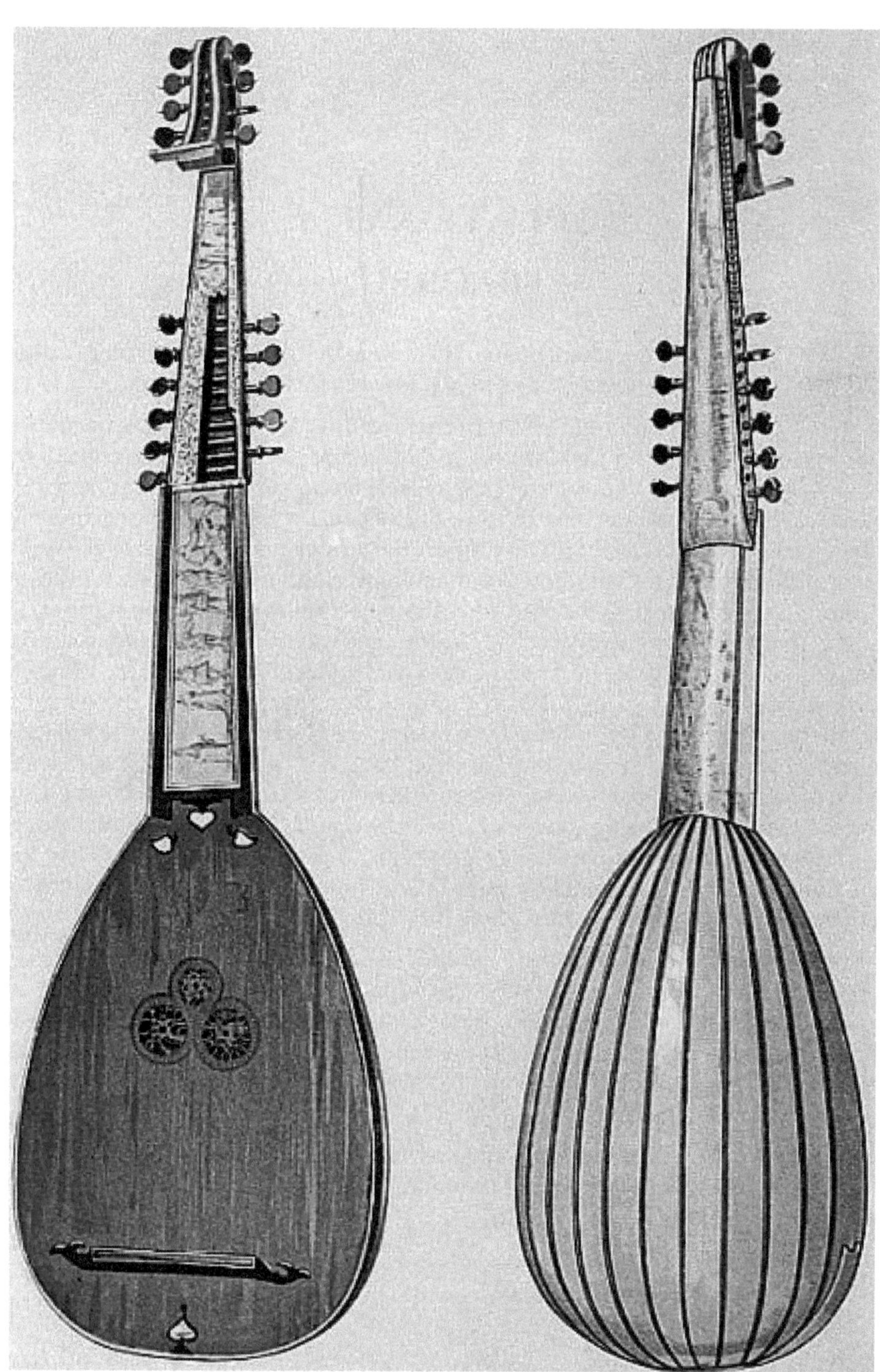

Plate XVI.

PLATE XVI.

THEORBO.

HE instrument here drawn was made by Giovanni Krebar of Padua in 1629, and now belongs to Mr. George Donaldson, London.

The body of this instrument is built up of ivory; the back of the peg-box and neck is also of ivory, and is delicately engraved with a view of Venice, showing vessels engaged in firing, and spearmen advancing. Incised dancing and fencing figures adorn the lower neck; there is a garden scene with numerous figures upon the upper neck. By the pegs we find the instrument had eight bass notes or diapasons; a single string to each note, and that there were on the finger-board five double strings and one, the highest, single—the chanterelle or melody string. In the true theorbo, the Paduan according to Baron (*Untersuchung des Instruments der Lauten*, Nuremberg, 1727, p. 131),—the diapasons were single strings. When the diapasons were in pairs of strings the instrument was, according to Mersenne (*Harmonie Universelle*, Paris, 1636), called (French) "Luth téorbé" or (Italian) "Liuto attiorbato," a theorboed lute. It must, however, be admitted that Mersenne's rule is not of strict application. The single strings introduced, in the first instance, for basses, at last became general throughout, and banished the double stringing in lutes, theorboes and guitars. The lutes were, however, by this time nearly out of use. The name Archlute is given by different authorities to both Theorbo and Chitarrone (Plate XXI.).

The early use of only one string for the highest or melody string may be seen in representations of lutes by Quattro Cento painters. The theorbo, however, was not introduced until nearly the end of the sixteenth century. A very accurate and beautiful painting of one may be observed in a picture by Terburg in the London National Gallery (formerly in the Peel Collection), which is erroneously named in the printed catalogue in use in 1887 "The Guitar Lesson."

Evelyn was well acquainted with the theorbo, and took lessons upon it in Rome and Padua. There is frequent mention of it in his Diary. It remained in use until nearly the end of the last century.

The extreme length of this specimen is 3 feet 5 inches; the body is 1 foot 3½ inches by nearly 11 inches.

Plate XVII.

PLATE XVII.

DULCIMER.

E derive "Dulcimer" from the Spanish "Dulcemele" as the only etymology to be offered with any show of certainty. The Provençal "Lai" was in the Latin of the period "Dulcis Cantus,"—"Dulcemele" (Lat. *Dulce Melos*) has a kindred ring, and by the change of a liquid "Dulcimer" has become an accepted name.

The dulcimer is a variety of the psaltery or *qanūn*, and bears the same relation to it that the modern pianoforte does to the older spinet or harpsichord. The psaltery was sounded by the fingers, either with their fleshy ends or by covering them with plectra adjusted like thimbles to produce a sharper sound; the dulcimer is a louder instrument, the sounds being produced by hammers held in the player's hands, and having elastic stems by which the necessary rebound from the strings is facilitated. The hammers have not unfrequently two coverings, a hard and a soft one, disposed upon the hammer head so that the player can, by turning the hammer, use either at will. The characteristic effect of the dulcimer, analogous to the mandoline, bandurria and other stringed instruments played with a plectrum, is the repetition of notes, producing by this artifice the impression of almost sustained sound. The Italians called the dulcimer "Salterio Tedesco," or German psaltery, but have now adopted Zimbalon; the Germans call it a "Hackbrett," or chopping board. It is generally an instrument popular among the humbler classes, and in modern times it assumes its most important rôle as the cimbalon in the Hungarian gipsy bands. The specimen here drawn belonged to Mr. Kendrick Pyne of Manchester, and is now in the possession of Mr. H. Boddington; it is elevated upon a stand, and is in a case, from which it can be removed for performance. There is a picture inside the lid of a sunset and figures habited in seventeenth-century costumes—soldiers advancing and met by ladies apparently bearing refreshments. On the front board, which is hinged so as to be let down, there is painted on the right of the spectator a man fishing in a pond and a woman near him; while in the centre is a clump of trees, and, on the left, a man and a woman meeting. The instrument itself is decorated with painted flowers in panels, between which are black and white chequers. It is probably Italian. The dimensions of it are—in the greatest width, 3 feet 4½ inches, in the least, 1 foot 11 inches. The angles of the sides measure 1 foot 1½ inch each. The depth of the instrument is 3½ inches. The height of the stand is 2 feet 2 inches.

There are seventeen notes of four wire strings tuned in unison for each note in this instrument. There may be more notes in a dulcimer and the number of strings may vary, groups of three, and even five unisons being found alternating with four in old dulcimers. The wire was brass in old instruments and is steel in modern ones. Owing to increase of tension due to the upward straining of the wire by the bridges on the sound-board, the places for the bridges cannot be determined by observing the simple ratios of partial tones, but have to be found empirically. As in all old stringed instruments there are sound-holes in the sound-board, in old Italian dulcimers decorated with beautiful arabesques or roses. In old Italian and also the Chinese dulcimers (Yang-ch'in, or foreign psaltery) the sound-board bridges are joined in two rows, the strings passing alternately over, and through openings made in them. They pass over brass wires on the summits of the bridges, and at the edges of the dulcimer over other brass wires that form, on either side, what may be called nuts. In Asiatic and modern European instruments the bridges are separate studs. The longest stretches of wire pass over the right-hand bridge and through the openings in the left-hand bridge. The shorter stretches are reversed, passing over the left-hand bridge. In European dulcimers the shorter stretches, struck to the right of the left-hand bridge, are an octave above the longer stretches struck to the left of the right-hand bridge. The shortest stretches are the remainder of the octave strings, which, carried over the left bridge to the left edge of the dulcimer, are so tuned as to be a fifth above the octave series. The right-hand remainder is not used. There are consequently three series of notes, a fundamental, an octave and a twelfth; thus expressed in notation, the perpendicular lines representing the nuts, and the circles the position of the bridges.

These are the lowest notes of the three series. The scale usually ascends from them in diatonic succession, in the lowest series with F natural instead of F sharp. In the last century attempts were made to tune some part of the scale chromatically, but, as far as I have met with examples, on no ascertainable system. The Chinese substitute sixths, and in the two lowest sevenths, for the octave; by the sevenths the lowest semitone is missed, otherwise the scale continues, as in the European dulcimer, in heptatonic order. The brass wire upon the bridges is an old spinet contrivance. The dulcimer is tuned with a hammer or key like a pianoforte, but, unlike the piano and other key-board instruments, has no damping contrivance.

We may look for the precursor of both the European and Chinese dulcimers in an Assyrian ancestor of the Persian Santir, or, it may be, in a more remote Babylonian instrument. Dulcimers are represented on Assyrian monuments.

Plate XVIII.

PLATE XVIII.

VIRGINAL.

N this interesting Virginal, which belongs to the Brussels Conservatoire, we have a Ruckers "Vierkante Clavisingel" in the original external decoration just as it left the hands of the younger Hans Ruckers, a master of the Saint Luke's Guild of Antwerp. The decoration is a covering of paper printed from blocks. The stand is also original. An untouched Ruckers virginal or harpsichord like this rarely comes under notice, and, at this moment, I can only recall one in England—a single key-board harpsichord in the possession of Miss Elizabeth Twining, at the Dial House, Twickenham, made by Andries, the brother of the younger Hans and, like him, a son of the elder Hans Ruckers.

The combination of white naturals and ebony sharps or flats is the oldest contrast between the lower and upper keys, with the qualification, that the oldest existing natural keys are not of ivory but of boxwood. As was customary in the Low Countries, Latin mottoes, sometimes more than one, were displayed on clavecins or key-board instruments. The one shown here reads OMNIS SPIRITVS LAVDET DOMINVM. These mottoes, so often occurring in Flemish instruments of that period, bear witness to the thoughtfulness and reverence of the men who made and possessed them. Besides the one quoted (Let all that breathe praise the Lord), we find LAVS DEO (Praise be to God), MVSICA DONVM DEI (Music is the gift of God), MVSICA MAGNORVM EST SOLAMEN DVLCE LABORVM (Music is the sweet solace to great labours), CONCORDIA RES PARVÆ CRESCVNT, DISCORDIA MAXIMÆ DILABVNTVR (By Concord small things grow, by Discord great things fall away), SIC TRANSIT GLORIA MVNDI (So passeth away the glory of the world), MVSICA LÆTITIÆ COMES MEDICINA DOLORVM (Music is the companion of joy and medicine of griefs), CONCORDIA MVSIS AMICA (Concord is the Muses' friend), ACTA VIRVM PROBANT (Deeds prove the man), SCIENTIA NON HABET INIMICVM NISI IGNORANTEM (Knowledge has no enemy but the ignorant), MVSICA PELLIT CVRAS (Music dispels cares), and SOLI DEO GLORIA (Glory be to God alone). The Italians preferred longer and more poetic quotations, as the often repeated "Viva fui in sylvis sum dura occisa securi; Dum vixi tacui mortua dulce cano" (I was alive in the woods, I was felled by a cruel axe; while I lived I was silent, now I am dead I sing sweetly); or that on the harpsichord which belonged to Tasso's sister, and is still in the possession of her descendants in the house she lived in at Sorrento: "Tales in altis sentiunt sonos beati spiritus opus" (Such sounds they hear in heaven, the blessed spirits' work).

To return to this Ruckers Virginal—the sound-board is painted with floral devices in Netherlandish fashion, the usual gilt rose appearing in the round opening of the sound-board, bearing the maker's trade mark, which contains his initials, I.R., and near it is written with ink, *Anno* 1622. Upon the rail above the jacks (plectra) is the inscription, JOANNES RVCKERS FECIT ANTVERPIÆ. There is a picture in the National Gallery in London, from the Peel Collection, painted by Metsu, wherein is depicted a precisely similar instrument, possibly his own, as he has it again in a picture belonging to the collection of Sir Francis Cook, at Richmond, in Surrey. At first sight it is difficult to believe it is not the same. Another occurs at Windsor Castle, in the collection of H.M. the Queen, painted by Ver Meer of Delft. Here, again, the first impression formed is that the painter has represented the instrument shown in the present drawing. Such Virginals must have been, at that time, favourite instruments in polite Dutch Society. Pepys, in his *Diary*, under date of September 2, 1666, has a well-known reference to the popularity of the virginal in London at the time of the Great Fire. "River full of lighters and boats taking in goods, and I observed that hardly one lighter or boat in three, that had the goods of a house in, but there was a pair of virginals in it." The word "virginals," here used, was evidently applied in a general sense, meaning any key-board plectrum instrument. The special virginal was an oblong spinet, and appears to have been the "spinetta," in the form invented by the Venetian Spinetti, about the year 1500. The Italian oblong spinet was furnished with a lid, the instrument being a fixture in the case. It presented to the eye the exact appearance of the cassone or wedding coffer, and was equally an object for decoration.

The rich sound of the Bass of the instrument here drawn, not soon to be forgotten, serves to show what the quality of tone throughout the scale must originally have been. It was this supreme excellence which raised the reputation of Hans Ruckers and his sons to a level to be rivalled only, later, by the great Cremona violin-makers; it lasted as long as the spinet and harpsichord remained in vogue.

This Virginal represents No. 15 of my Catalogue of existing Ruckers instruments in Sir George Grove's *Dictionary of Music and Musicians*, article "Ruckers." London, 1883.

The woodcuts above the Contents to this work represent Sir Michael Mercator (1491-1544), a musical instrument maker, it is said virginal maker, to King Henry VIII. The portrait has been engraved from a medal in the British Museum executed by Mercator himself, for he was a goldsmith and medallist as well as instrument maker, by Mr. John Hipkins, who has also engraved the Jewish Shophar and the woodcut on the title-page. The legend upon the medal informs us that Mercator was the first knight created from Venloo by the King. He gained knighthood and other distinctions by his success in secret diplomatic services. The researches of Mr. W.H. James Weale, who called the attention of the present writer to Mercator, have determined his arrival in this country to have been in 1527, when he brought letters of introduction to Cardinal Wolsey from Floris d'Egmont, Count de Buren and Lord of Isselstein, and others, and two musical instruments—as he was an organ-builder, it is to be presumed virginals. The King engaged him at an annual salary. It will be observed in the portrait that Mercator wears, attached to his collar, the Tudor Rose. Mr. Weale has published his discoveries concerning him in *Le Beffroi*, an artistic and antiquarian periodical printed at Bruges. Mr. Weale's Descriptive Catalogue of the rare manuscripts and printed books in the Historical Music Loan Collection of 1885, for the publication of which we are indebted to Mr. Bernard Quaritch, may be appropriately mentioned in this connection.

Plate XIX.

PLATE XIX.

VIOLA DA GAMBA.

THE old Bass Viol (French *Basse de Viole*) derives its name of Viola da Gamba (leg viol) from its having been held between the knees of the player, whence the German "Kniegeige." Shakspeare speaks of it as "viol-de-gamboys" in *Twelfth Night*—where Sir Toby Belch in his panegyric on Sir Andrew Aguecheek says, "He plays o' the viol-de-gamboys, and speaks three or four languages word for word without book, and hath all the good gifts of nature." Domenichino's famous St. Cecilia is represented as playing upon a viola da gamba. It was the bass of the chest (or family) of viols. A quotation from the recently published autobiography of the Honourable Roger North, who was born in 1653, aptly describes the domestic use of those once admired instruments. He says his grandfather, Dudley, third Lord North, when at his country seat in Norfolk, "would convoke his musical family ... and for important regale of the company the concerts were usually all viols to the organ or harpsichord. The violin came in late and imperfectly. When the hands were well supplied the whole chest went to work, that is six viols, music being formed for it which would seem a strange sort of music now, being an interwoven hum-drum." Roger North became himself a proficient upon both treble and bass viols.

The splendid example here drawn is the work of Joachim Tielke, who made it at Hamburg in 1701; it formerly belonged to the famous violoncellist, F. Servais. In perfect preservation, it has a beautifully carved ivory peg-box, which is surmounted by a woman's head, with an incised finger-board beneath. There are no frets, which is unusual with viols, as they were fretted instruments, but it would be of course easy to attach them. The back is of rosewood alternated with ivory; and the ivory tailpiece forms a caduceus. Two views are given of the instrument, and a profile of the head and peg-box are enlarged to half size. It has six strings, a favourite accordance being—

This was called the Harp-way sharp; when the fifth string was tuned to B flat the tuning was called Harp-way flat—Harp-way, indicating the facility thus afforded for arpeggios.

Bach's solemn cantata, "Gottes Zeit ist die allerbeste Zeit" (God's time is the best of all times), opens with the viola da gamba, but, early in the eighteenth century, composers replaced the Viola da Gamba with the violoncello. The last noted performer upon it was Carl Friedrich Abel, who died in 1787. Of late years it has been taken up again for its own special qualities, which should preserve it for at least occasional use. The late Henry Webb, at the suggestion of Professor Ernst Pauer in 1862, was perhaps the first to adopt it again. He had to obtain instruction in the fingering of the instrument from an old man of eighty-six. The fingering is practically that of the lute, and, as Mr. E.J. Payne has pointed out in Grove's *Dictionary of Music and Musicians* (Art. "Violin"), it was the command of the six-stringed finger-board which the lutenists had attained by two centuries of incessant practice that was transferred by them to the Viola da Gamba, both instruments being thus common to the same players. Owing to this fact the bass viol remained in use much longer than the other members of the viol family. At the present time Mr. Payne, Herr Paul de Wit of Leipsic, and Mr. E. Jacobs of Brussels, have reintroduced the Viola da Gamba to the notice of the musical public. Mr. Jacobs played upon one furnished with sympathetic strings, with great success in the Historical Concerts given, under the direction of Mr. Victor Mahillon, in the Music Room of the London International Inventions Exhibition of 1885. The instrument here represented belongs to the Museum of the Brussels Conservatoire.

Plate XX.

PLATE XX.

DOUBLE SPINET OR VIRGINAL.

HIS uncommon instrument displays one of the expedients employed to gain a more brilliant effect by the addition of an octave string, before such a string was permanently attached to the sound-board of the harpsichord itself by means of an additional row of strings placed beneath the ordinary unison strings. Octave spinets were, as Mersenne (1636) describes, made independent of the ordinary spinet, and there are frequent examples to be met with. These little spinets were placed upon the larger ones for performance, as Praetorius (1619) says, like turrets on a tower. In this double spinet it is a removable part of the instrument, and constitutes the left-hand key-board, the right-hand key-board being a fixture. The maker, as is proved by his initials, H R, and his device in the rose of the sound-hole, is no other than the famous Hans Ruckers the elder, of Antwerp. This Spinet is numbered 9 of the sixty-six existing instruments by the Ruckers family catalogued by the present writer in Sir George Grove's *Dictionary of Music and Musicians*. It can now be extended to sixty-eight. On the jack rails of both spinets may be read "Joannes Rvqvers me fecit." There is another double spinet at Nuremberg made in 1580 by Martin Vander Beest, which has been figured and is the frontispiece to Dr. August Reissmann's *Illustrirte Geschichte der Deutschen Musik* (Leipzig, 1881). The Ruckers double spinet can hardly be much later. The earliest examples known to me of the octave string attached, as above mentioned, in the harpsichord itself, are to be found in a double clavecin (French for harpsichord) by Hans Ruckers the elder, dated 1590, and preserved in the Museum of the Paris Conservatoire, and in a clavicembalo (Italian for harpsichord), made at Pesaro, and also in 1590,—lately brought to England by Messrs. Hill, the violin-makers, and now acquired by the South Kensington Museum. The latter is an instrument with only two strings to each note. The invention of the octave string, as well as of double key-board, has been attributed to Hans Ruckers. The latest evidence, however, does not favour these attributions, although both inventions most likely belong to the Netherlands. Ruckers and his sons, it may be said, made instruments that were never surpassed for quality of tone. To return to the Double Spinet—both key-boards are of four octaves, the fixed right-hand one being from the second C below, to the second above, middle C, and the removable left-hand one is an octave higher throughout. The complete instrument rests upon the original arcaded stand.

The paintings are of later date than the instrument itself. The subjects are on the lid, and represent a contest before the gods between Apollo and Marsyas—the former divinity playing a viol, and the latter a pipe. The background is a hilly country with a lake and castle, and a man in a boat. Above and below the removable spinet are painted landscapes with figures, immediately above it children dancing; and at the fixed key-board men and women dancing in pairs. This pleasing instrument formerly belonged to Messrs. Chappell of London, but is now the property of Mr. George Donaldson.

There are seven pierced arches and columns in the stand, which is 2 feet 4 inches high. The dimensions are—extreme length, 5 feet 8½ inches; the length of the left-hand key-board, 2 feet 2½ inches, and of the right-hand one, 2 feet 1¼ inches. The width from back to front is 1 foot 7½ inches, and the depth is 11½ inches.

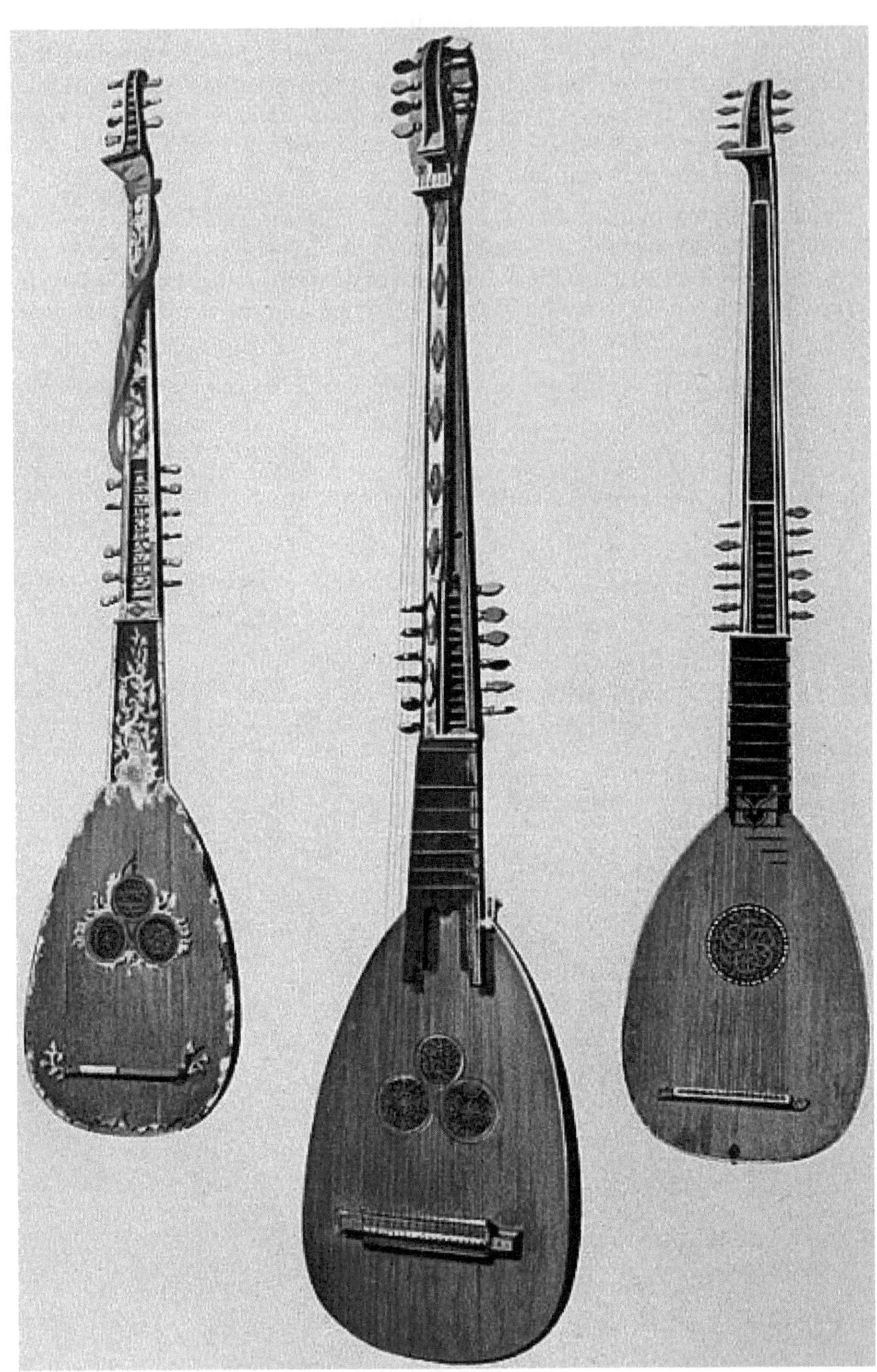

Plate XXI.

PLATE XXI.

THREE CHITARRONI.

HE primary meaning of "Chitarrone" is a large guitar, but, in point of fact, this imposing yet graceful instrument is a theorbo or bass lute with a very long upper neck to give length for bass strings of deep pitch. The one to the left in the drawing, which belongs to Mr. Rudolf Lehmann, London, is Venetian, if we may judge from the beautiful decoration. It has three sound-holes with roses joined together in a fashion that is regarded as Roman, and is adorned with mother of pearl. It is strung with six pairs of strings upon the finger-board, each pair tuned in unison. Seven single diapason strings, or open basses, are stretched from the upper peg-box clear of the finger-board. It is 5 feet in extreme length, that of the neck being 3 feet 5 inches. The Chitarrone in the centre, which belongs to Mr. George Donaldson, and is richly inlaid with mother of pearl, has also three connected roses, six pairs of unisons upon the finger-board and eight diapasons clear of it. The length of it is 6 feet; the neck is 4 feet 1 inch. It is also Venetian, and dated 1608. The right-hand Chitarrone, shown at the Exhibition of 1885 by Mr. Edward Joseph of Bond Street, London, has six pairs of unisons and seven diapasons. The neck is ornamented with chequers, and the finger-board is bound with thirteen frets for the melody strings, giving the player a semitone more than the complete chromatic series.

The chitarrone is sometimes called the Roman theorbo. It is of greater length than the Paduan theorbo, with which it was introduced towards the end of the sixteenth century,—owing to a necessity having arisen for bass instruments of greater sonorousness than had been used before, in order to accompany the newly-invented recitative. About the same time there also came into use a larger instrument of the viol family, known as the violone, the precursor of the double bass. The heavier basses and simple harmonies, for which the Italians had shown a growing preference, replaced, to a great extent, the ingenious interweavings of counterpoint, and assisted the development of the latest offspring of the Renaissance, that of Monody—the recitativo and aria—introduced in Florence by Peri, Caccini, Cavalieri and Monteverde, the foundation of the modern Italian opera.

The chitarrone was used in the orchestra of Monteverde on the first production of his *Orfeo* in 1607. There is also mention of it in a band of instruments as early as 1589.

Plate XXII.

PLATE XXII.

SPINET.

THIS "Spinet," with its original six-legged stand, was made in London about the end of the seventeenth century. "Stephanus Keene Londini Fecit," is inscribed upon the name-board, which is characteristically inlaid with birds and foliage. It is a transverse Spinet, the Italian "Spinetta traversa," an adaptation of the longer bichord or trichord harpsichord within the limitations of size of this instrument, which, like the trapeze-shaped and oblong spinets, had one string only to each note. The tail is extended on the right-hand side; the key-board is placed somewhat obliquely, and the wrest-plank, with the tuning-pins, is immediately above the key-board, instead of being, as in the older spinets, at the right-hand side. The compass of the key-board is from the second B below, to the second D above, the middle C,—in all four octaves and two notes, being one note more in the treble than occurs in the key-board diagram to Henry Purcell's *Lessons for the Harpsichord or Spinnet*. The lowest key would, however, be tuned down to the lowest pianoforte G, the object being to secure a dominant bass for the lowest C. Purcell's diagram for the spinet gives the lowest key as "B B," but, in the lessons, he here and there writes down to G G, also to A A, for which the lowest C♯ key would be similarly accommodated. The two lowest sharps of the spinet here drawn present the peculiarity of being cut or divided, each division being an independent key. These were not quarter-tones as has been supposed; the front halves were tuned A and B for dominant basses like the G, and the back halves C♯ and D♯, chromatic semitones to the adjacent natural notes, thus combining the "Short Octave" principle, indispensable for the performance of contemporary music, with the chromatic system then beginning to be recognised.

Stephen Keene was a well-known maker of spinets, equal in reputation to his great rivals, Charles Haward, and Thomas and John Hitchcock. The earliest notice known of Keene occurs in an advertisement at the end of the sixth edition of Playford's Introduction (London, 1671), which announces that "Mr. George Dalham, that excellent organ-maker, dwelleth now in Purple-Lane, next door to the Crooked Billet, where such as desire to have new organs, or old mended, may be well accommodated."

"And Mr. Stephen Keene, Maker of Harpsycons and Virginals, dwelleth now in Threadneedle-Street, at the sign of the Virginal, who maketh them exactly good, both for sound and substance."

It is proved that Keene was long in business by a name-board which is in my possession dated 1719. Indeed, longer than the period occupied by Thomas Hitchcock, whose autograph occurs in spinets from 1664 and 1703. The principal dimensions of the instrument drawn, which belongs to Mr. H.J. Dale, Cheltenham, are—extreme width, 5 feet 6 inches, extreme depth, without the projection of the key-board, 1 foot 9¼ inches. The key-board is 2 feet 4¼ inches wide, and 3⅞ inches deep.

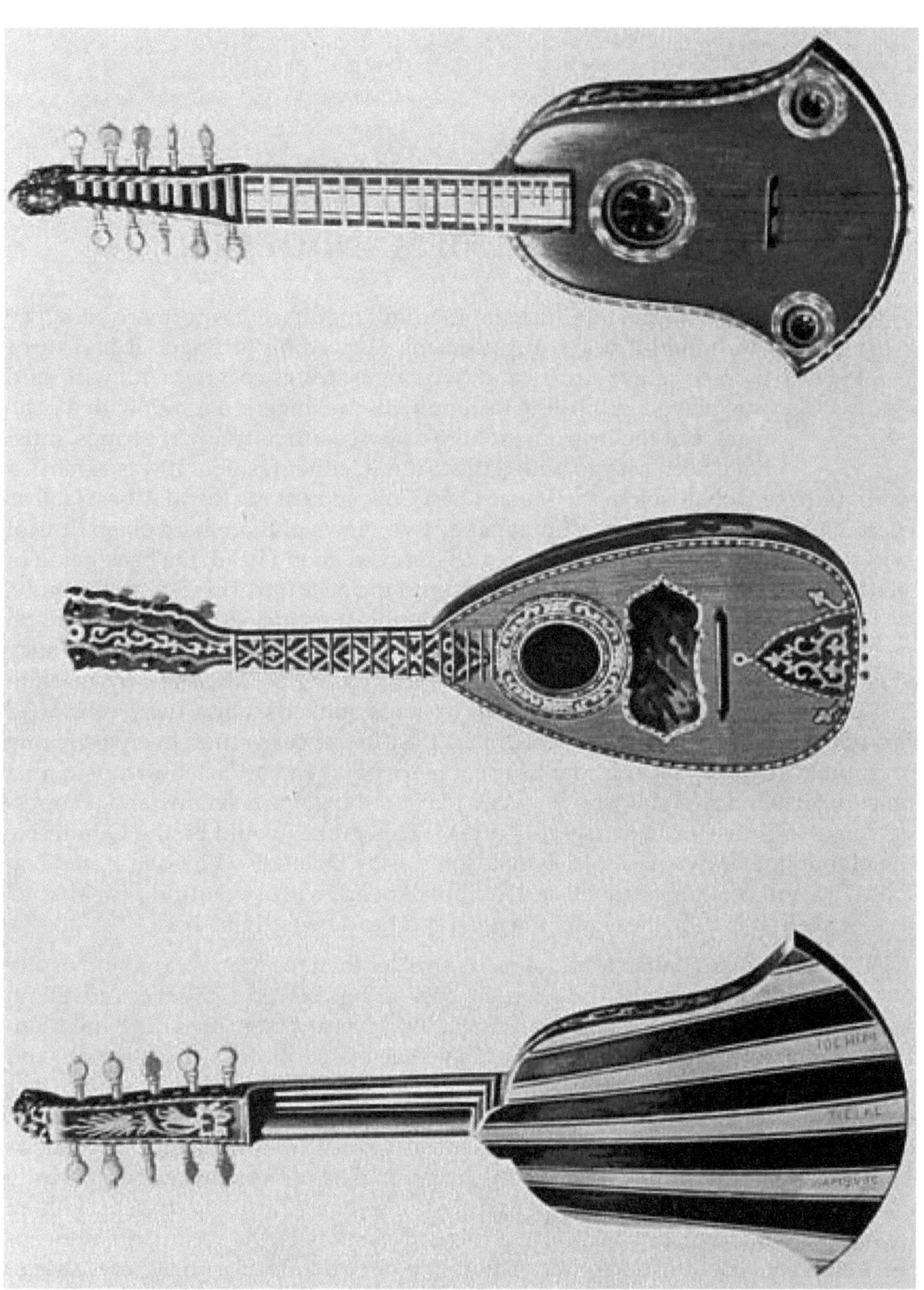

Plate XXIII.

PLATE XXIII.

QUINTERNA AND MANDOLINE.

HE Quinterna or Chiterna, the Italian guitar, was formerly used by the humbler order of musicians. According to Engel, it had three pairs of catgut strings and two single strings covered with wire, and was played guitar-lute fashion with the fingers, and not with a plectrum. But the instrument here drawn, with its ten wire strings, must have been played with a plectrum in cither fashion. It was exhibited by Mr. George Donaldson in the Music Loan Collection at the Royal Albert Hall as a Giterna, an obvious variant of the name. Two views of it are here given. It is of tortoiseshell with arabesques of ivory and a carved ebony head, the back being of ebony and ivory. In length it is 24½ inches, and the neck, measured from the body, is 14 inches. The words, "Joachim Tielke Hamburg fecit, 1676," are inscribed on the back of the instrument; the date, however, suggests a considerable discrepancy when compared with the Quinterna in South Kensington Museum, by Joachim Tielke, 1539. Engel supposes that this famous maker's name was continued through several generations, to account for the difference in dates. Evelyn, visiting Pozzuoli in 1645, says, "The country-people so jovial and addicted to musiq, that the very husbandmen almost universaly play on the guitarr, singing and composing songs in praise of their sweet-heartes." This guitar would be the Quinterna. The Mandoline drawn, also Mr. Donaldson's, is by Domenico Vinaccia, dated Napoli, 1780, and is of tortoiseshell and mother of pearl, with a beautiful pear-shaped back or shell. It is 22 inches long, the neck and head being 11 inches.

The Mandoline (Italian Mandolino) is smaller than the Mandora, a kind of alto lute. It is strung with catgut and wire, the bass strings being of catgut covered with silver wire, and is played with a plectrum. Of several kinds, including the Mandore, Mandurina, and Pandurina, that have been used in Italy, the Milanese and Neapolitan Mandolines are the best known. The Milanese Mandoline, with five or six pairs of strings, preserves old cither tunings; the Neapolitan Mandoline, which is really an eighteenth-century instrument, is evidently of later introduction, as it is tuned in fifths similar to a violin, which makes performance upon it easily attainable by violin players. Mozart wrote the serenade in *Don Giovanni* with an accompaniment for it, but beautiful as this composition is, the accompaniment appears scarcely characteristic of the Mandoline or of the Bandurria either—a small kind of Spanish guitar of deeper pitch than the Mandoline, which, for local colour, would have been the right instrument. These instruments, like the Dulcimer, make their characteristic effects by means of the reiteration of notes, analogous to what is called "repetition" on a pianoforte, the intention being to convey an impression of sustained sound, and make the melody prominent when several other instruments are being played.

The accordance of the Neapolitan Mandoline is—

of the Milanese Mandoline of five notes—

of the Milanese Mandoline of six notes—

and of the Bandurria—

the three higher notes being here of catgut—the lower of silk overspun with metal. The Bandurria, like the Mandolines, is played with a plectrum, called in Spanish "Pua," which is prevented from defacing the wood by the presence of a tortoise-shell plate, let into the sound-board. The plectrum is usually a small piece of tortoiseshell or quill.

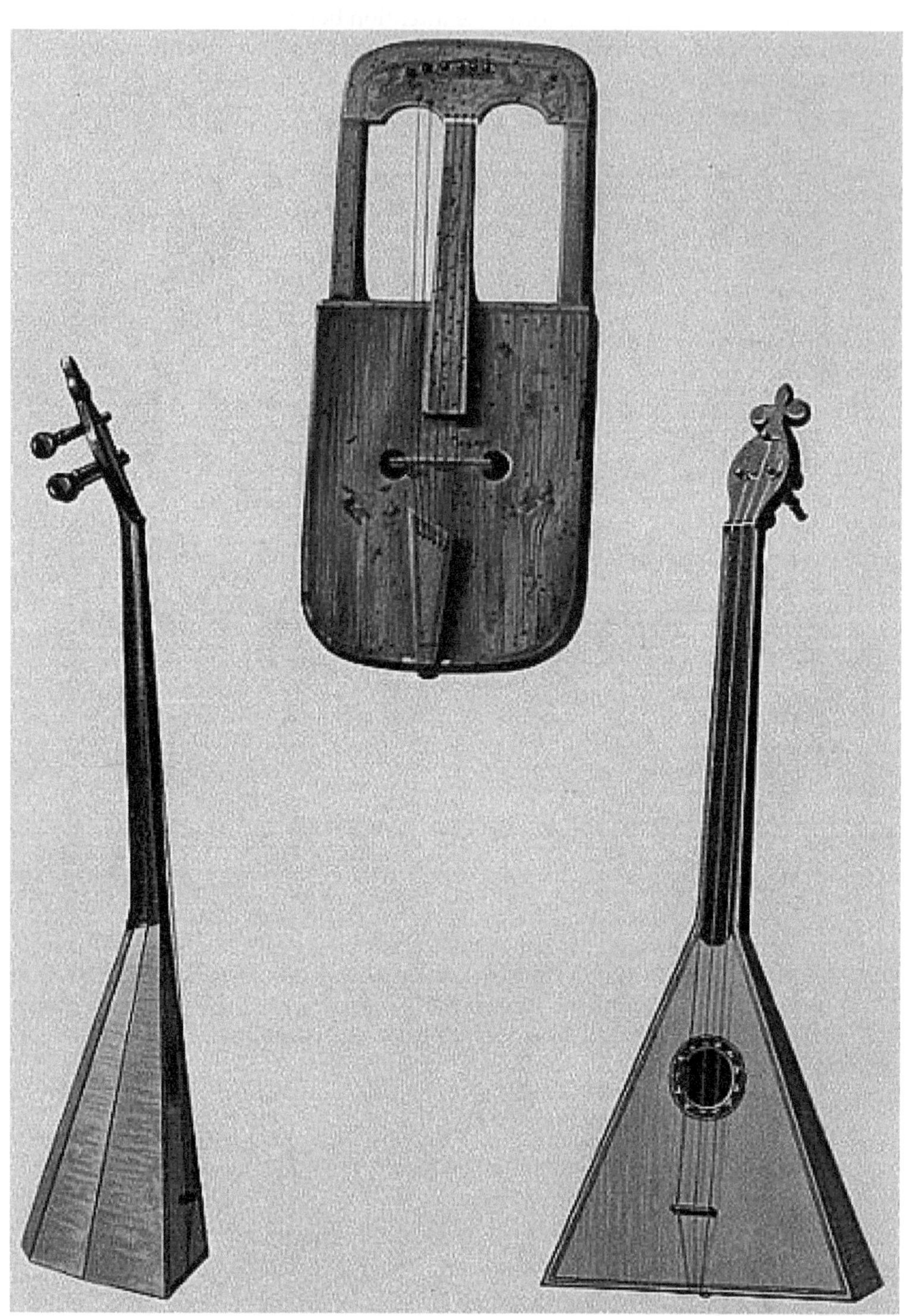

Plate XXIV.

PLATE XXIV.

WELSH CRWTH. RUSSIAN BALALÄIKA.

THE Crwth is a rare Welsh instrument, supposed to have been the "Chrotta Brittanna" mentioned in one of the odes of Venantius Fortunatus, written about A.D. 617, and published under the title of "Venantii Fortunati Poemata"; but following the analogy of the Gaelic "cruith," and the phonetic "crot" of the Book of the Dean of Lismore (a sixteenth-century collection of Ossianic fragments), the British Chrotta was more likely to have been an early form of the Celtic Harp. Of original Welsh Crwths known there are three—one from the Engel collection in the South Kensington Museum, another less perfect in the Warrington Museum, and the one here drawn, which belongs to Colonel Wynne-Finch of Voelas, Bettws-y-Coed, North Wales. They have been hollowed out of single pieces of wood, the sound-board being glued on—a very primitive manner of structure akin to the old Celtic Harps. The dimensions of Colonel Wynne-Finch's Crwth are—length, 22½ inches; width, between 10½ and 9 inches; depth, 2 inches. This instrument has six strings, although nearer examination shows that it had originally only five; four are on a finger-board played with a bow, and two are off the finger-board, intended to be twanged by the player's thumb. These open strings are a comparatively late fancy, adopted in the theorbo, lyra, and baryton viols. It is said there was a three-stringed crwth (Crwth thrithant) probably bowed, and tuned as the first, fifth, and octave, but I am disposed to agree with the late Carl Engel (*Researches into the Early History of the Violin Family*: London, 1883) that this could be no other than the mediæval Rebec. From observations made, more than a hundred years ago, by the Hon. Daines Barrington (published in the *Archæologia* of the Society of Antiquaries, London, Vol. III. p. 20), who had the advantage of hearing a performer claiming to be the last upon the instrument, the accordance of the six-stringed crwth was—

The strings were of catgut. Another authority, Bingley, heard the crwth played at Carnarvon as late as 1801. He gives a different accordance, in which, however,

the octave arrangement remains:—

It would appear as if the notes forming octaves upon the finger-board were bowed together but not all four strings at once, as has been sometimes supposed. To effect this there must have been a peculiar knack in using the bow. From the large openings on either side of the finger-board it is possible to trace, through the intermediate mediæval Rotta or Rote, a descent from the Græco-Roman Cythara or Lyre. There are two sound-holes in the belly, and the bridge, which is placed obliquely, has the right foot resting upon the belly, while the left foot, as in the tromba marina, passes through the left sound-hole to rest upon the back. The left foot then acts as a sound-post, and sets the whole instrument in vibration. Colonel Wynne-Finch's Crwth was found in the Island of Anglesey. It has the following inscription upon a label inside:—

MAID IN THE PARIS OF
ANIRHENGEL BY RICHARD
EVANS INSTRUMENTS MAKER
IN THE YEAR 1742.

But it is supposed to be older, and only to have been repaired or reconstructed by Richard Evans. It was restored very carefully by Mr. George Chanot before being shown at South Kensington in the Loan Collection of 1872.

The BALALÄIKA is the Russian peasant's guitar. This example was drawn because of the ornament, but the common instrument is usually quite plain. It came from Moscow tuned  but another in my possession, sent to me at the same time from St. Petersburg, was tuned . The Balaläika has three frets attached to the neck, for stopping the semitone, whole tone, and minor third on each string. The strings are of catgut. The quality of tone is very sympathetic, almost sad.

The dimensions of the specimen drawn are—extreme height from the base, 30 inches; the finger-board, 13 inches; the width at base is 11½ inches. The depth of the sound-chest, which is the half of a duodecagon, 5¾ inches. The corresponding measures of the simple peasant's instruments are—26¾, 13¾, 13, and 3½ inches.

The peculiar triangular shape of the Balaläika is of very primitive character, the curved form in lutes and guitars being an artistic development. In a delightfully realistic Russian bronze shown at the Health Exhibition, South Kensington,

1884, the performer simultaneously holds the neck of the instrument and stops the strings with his left hand, while he touches them, guitar fashion, with his right hand, the instrument being free from any other support whatever.

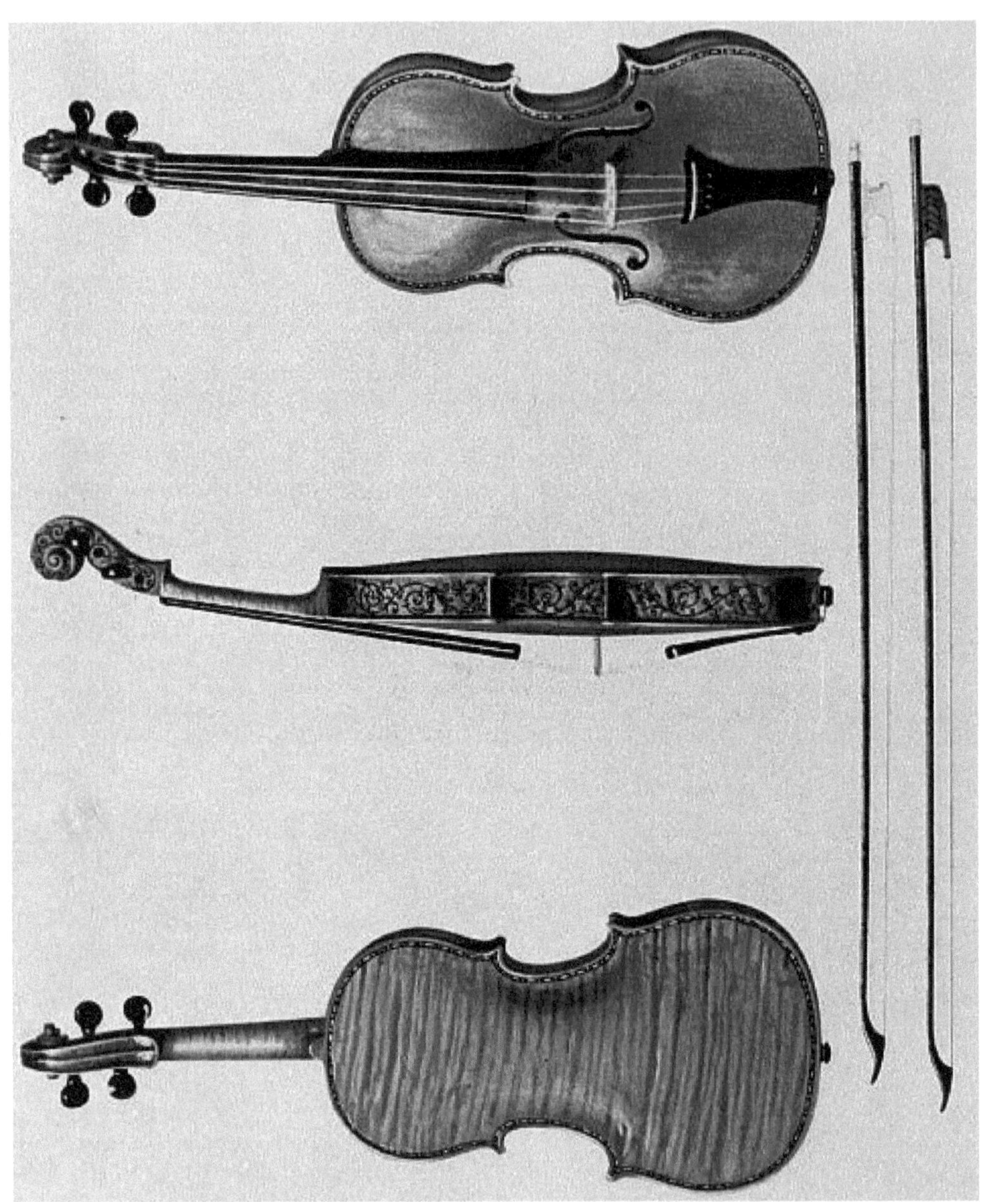

Plate XXV.

PLATE XXV.

VIOLIN, THE HELLIER STRADIVARIUS, AND TWO OLD BOWS NOTED FOR THE FLUTING.

HIS is the beautiful "Hellier" Stradivarius Violin made in 1679 and bought by Sir Samuel Hellier of Womborne, Staffordshire, about the year 1734, from the maker himself. It remained in the Hellier family until 1875, when it was acquired by Mr. George Crompton, who subsequently disposed of it to Messrs. W.E. Hill and Sons of New Bond Street, formerly of Wardour Street, London, the experts in the violin section of the South Kensington Music Loan Collection of 1885. It now belongs to Mr. Charles Oldham, who possesses another inlaid violin dated 1687, which was originally made for the King of Spain, and completes his quartet of Stradivarius instruments. This Violin is considered to be one of the perfect earlier works of Stradivarius, and is of full proportions. It has greater breadth than the so-called "grand" pattern of that famous maker, and is one of his inlaid violins, of which there are not more than twelve extant. A letter of Stradivarius, recording the price (£40) Sir Samuel Hellier paid for it, was forthcoming until a few years ago, when it was unfortunately lost. We are not informed why Stradivarius should have kept this instrument in his own possession for fifty-five years—it seems likely that it had had another owner before Sir Samuel Hellier, and that Stradivarius had taken it back. The details of the ornament upon this Violin have been corrected from an exact tracing taken by Mrs. Huggins of Upper Tulse Hill, London, an earnest amateur of Stradivari's violins. The Hellier Stradivarius was certainly one of the most remarkable examples that appeared in the unrivalled collection of famous violins exhibited at South Kensington in 1885.

A quotation from Mr. George Hart's well-known book upon *The Violin, its Famous Makers and their Imitators* (London, 1884, p. 191), justly sums up the worth of those artificers when Italian violin-making most excelled. He says: "The chief merits of Stradivari and his contemporary makers were intuitive. Their rules, having their origin in experience, were applied as dictated by their marvellous sense of touch and cunning, with results infinitely superior to any obtained with the aid of the most approved mechanical contrivances. When to these considerations we add that devotedness of purpose without which nothing great in art has been accomplished, we have a catalogue of excellences sufficient to account for the greatness of their achievements."

The bows that accompany the "Hellier" Stradivarius are from the collection of Messrs. Arthur and Alfred Hill. The violin bow, the medium by which the performer's personality is transmitted to the instrument and its various powers are brought out, is not less worthy of admiration than the violin itself. The gradual improvement of the bow has followed the development and improvement of the violin, and the settlement of its form and materials in the last quarter of the last century by François Tourte, in reality made the violin a different instrument from what it had been before. With Tourte's bow came a power of expression in violin-playing previously unknown.

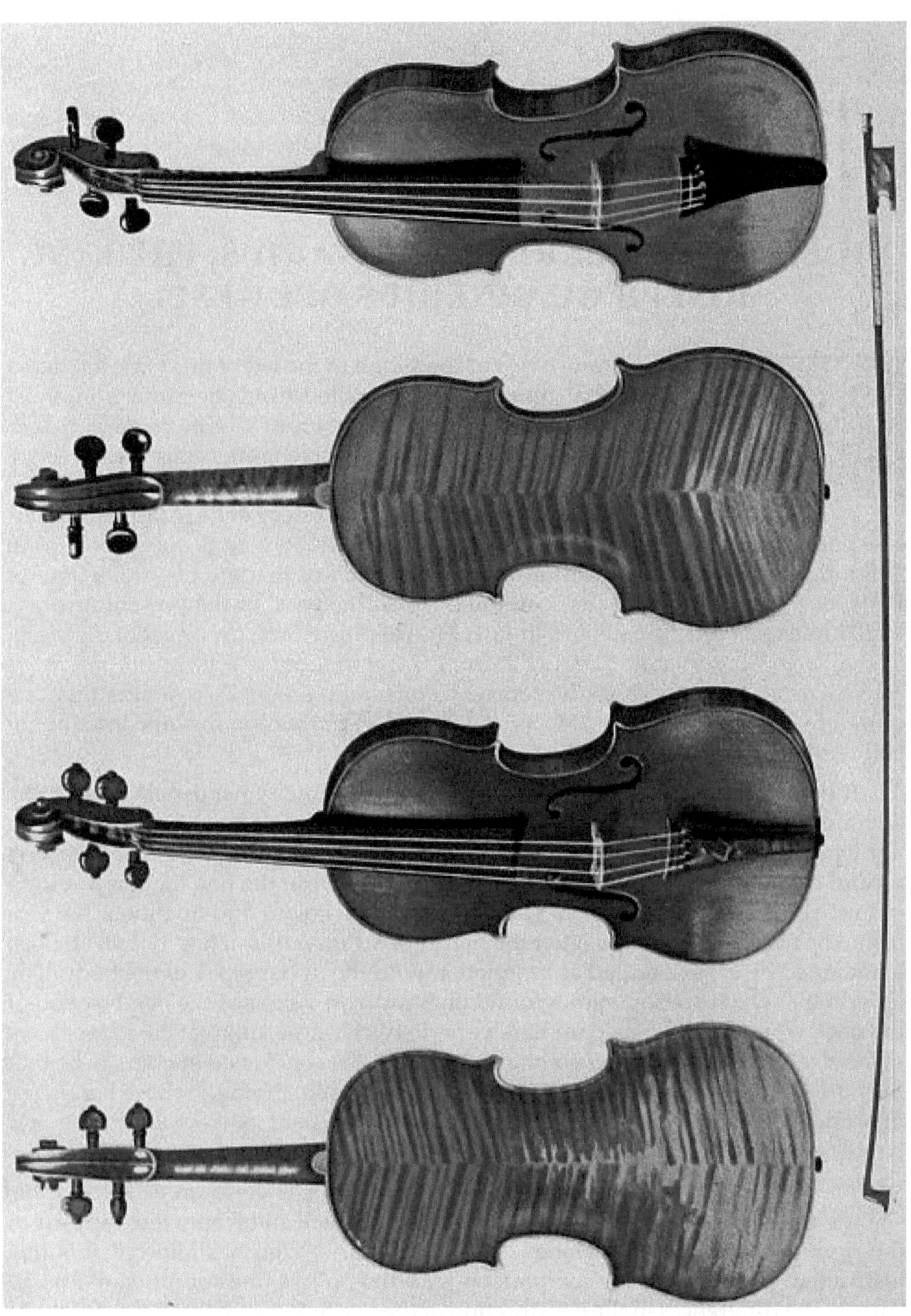

Plate XXVI.

PLATE XXVI.

VIOLINS, THE ALARD STRADIVARIUS, THE KING JOSEPH GUARNERIUS DEL GESÙ.

HE back and front views of the Violin to the left of this Plate are taken from the "Alard" Stradivarius, so called from the famous violinist who formerly owned it. It is one of the finest violins made by Stradivarius, and bears the date 1715, thus belonging to his great period, which is considered by connoisseurs to have extended from about 1700 to 1725. The following is the brief history of the Alard Stradivarius. Bought in Florence early in the present century by a banker of Courtrai in Belgium, it passed at his death into the possession of the late J.B. Vuillaume of Paris, one of the most famous violin-makers and experts of the present century. Vuillaume reserved it for his son-in-law, Mr. Delphin Alard, professor of the violin at the Paris Conservatoire, and of European reputation as a virtuoso, in whose possession it remained until he retired from public life in 1876. It was then acquired by Mr. David Laurie of Glasgow, in whose possession this fine instrument still remains.

It is a Stradivarius of the "grand" form, and of a very handsome model, the arching of the belly and back being of exquisite proportions, neither exaggerated nor weak. The workmanship is between the earlier and later styles of the master. A careful choice of the wood is of course presupposed, but the fine regular marking of the back may be observed, and also the beautiful colour and quality of the varnish. The neck is original, as it left the hands of Stradivarius; it has, however, been lengthened by a piece added at its junction with the upper block of the body. The letters P.S., which are sometimes found on Stradivari violins at the peg-box end of the neck when it is original, are here very distinct. These enigmatical letters have given rise to some discussion among experts, but the conclusion appears to be that they are the initials of Stradivari's youngest son, Paolo, through whose hands the instruments may have passed. Paolo was a cloth merchant, not a violin-maker, but he succeeded to his father's house after the decease of his brothers.

The "King Joseph" Guarnerius del Gesù Violin (del Gesù on account of his signing his violins with the device I.H.S.), of which back and front views appear to the right of the Plate, also belongs to Mr. Laurie, who has allowed this fine instrument to be drawn for comparison with the no less fine specimen of Stradivarius. The differences in the construction of the instruments of these famous makers are, to the practised eye, considerable. In general, the violins of Guarneri are smaller than those of Stradivari. There is a marked difference observable in the outlines of the two makers, the Stradivarius being somewhat square in the shoulders, the C's, or inward curvings of the sides of a violin which resemble that letter, and in the lower part, while all those features in the Guarnerius are more curved. The head of the latter is bolder, less symmetrical and quaintly original. The "*f*'s," the sound-holes in violins assuming the form of that letter as an italic, which are beautifully curved by Stradivarius, are by Guarnerius often sharply pointed at top and bottom. It might be expected that this peculiarity of the "*f*'s" would be detrimental to the artistic effect, but it is not. The arching of the belly and back is with Guarnerius less marked than with Stradivarius. Generally speaking, Guarnerius left his bellies thicker than those of Stradivarius. As may be expected, there is a decided difference in tone between a Guarnerius del Gesù and a Stradivarius. I am indebted to Dr. William Huggins, F.R.S., for the following interesting comparison. The Stradivarius possesses, as a rule, a brighter tone with unlimited capacity for expressing the most varied accents of feeling, "welling forth like a spring (says Dr. Joachim in Mr. Payne's 'Stradivari,' Grove's *Dictionary*, vol. iii., p. 733) and capable of infinite modifications under the bow." The tone of Guarnerius has intense individuality, it is powerful and somewhat contralto in quality, with a superb mellow richness strongly tinged with melancholy.

The famous "King Joseph" Guarnerius del Gesù was formerly in the celebrated collection formed by the late James Goding. It was sold after his decease in 1857 to the Viscomte de Janzé, from whom Mr. Laurie obtained it. The Tourte bow, mounted with gold, tortoiseshell and mother of pearl, shown in the same Plate, is also Mr. Laurie's.

Plate XXVII.

PLATE XXVII.

VIOLA D'AMORE.

FRENCH "La Viole d'Amour" is the Love Viol, so called from the soft and tender quality of the tone produced from it. Beneath the catgut strings there are usually wire strings, which, being tuned in accordance, vibrate sympathetically when the catgut strings are bowed. This is in obedience to a well-known law of physics, according to which a body set in vibration will cause another body having the same frequency of vibration to sound when within reach of its influence. In the beautifully carved and inlaid instrument here drawn, a perfect viola d'amore in form, surmounted by a lovely head with bandaged eyes, the sympathetic strings are absent, and if they were ever attached the peg-box has since been altered. But it has the "flaming sword" sound-holes invariably found in a viola d'amore, and also the addition, not unfrequent in that viol, of a rose immediately under the finger-board.

Meyerbeer has revived the use of the viola d'amore by writing for it the delicious *obbligato* to Raoul's song, "Ah! quel spectacle enchanteur," in *Les Huguenots.* In the present day Mr. Carli Zoeller has come forward in England as the regenerator of the viola d'amore. He has published an instruction-book, with an historical introduction of value, and has also composed for the instrument. The following interesting passage occurs in John Playford's *Musick's Recreation on the Viol Lyra-way,* London, 1661:—"The first authors of inventing and setting lessons this way to the Viol was Mr. *Daniel Farunt,* Mr. *Alfonso Ferabosco,* and Mr. *John Coperario* alias *Cooper*. The first of these was a person of much ingenuity for his several rare inventions of instruments, as the Poliphant and the Stump, which were strung with wire; and also of his last, which was a *Lyra Viol,* strung with Lute strings and Wire strings, the one above the other; the wire strings were conveyed through a hollow passage made in the neck of the Viol and so brought to the tail thereof, and raised a little above the belly of the viol by a bridge of about ½ an inch. These were so laid that they were equivalent to those above, and were tun'd unisons to those above, so that by striking of those strings above with the bow, a sound was drawn from those of wire underneath, which made it very harmonious; of this sort of Viols I have seen many, but Time and Disuse have set them aside." This description may have referred to the Viola Bastarda, with the invention of which Praetorius credits England. A great authority on this subject, Mr. E.J. Payne, writing in Sir George Grove's *Dictionary of Music and Musicians* (article Violin), says the principle of sympathetic vibration was applied to several Viols, even the little Sordino. The Viola

Bastarda was the Viola da Gamba with wire strings added. In the same way the Tenor Viol became the usual Viola d'Amore. But the latter has varied in construction, the name being applied by Mattheson (1713) to a Viol with four metal strings and one of catgut, which he said bore "the beautiful name of Viola d'Amore (Viole d'Amour), in fact, for it expresses much languishment and tenderness." This must have been similar to the Viola d'Amore "of 5 wyre strings plaied on with a bow," described by Evelyn in 1679 as "above all for its sweetnesse and novelty."

The tuning of the Viola d'Amore was at first the ordinary viol way of fourths and a third, but later the major common chord tuning was given to it

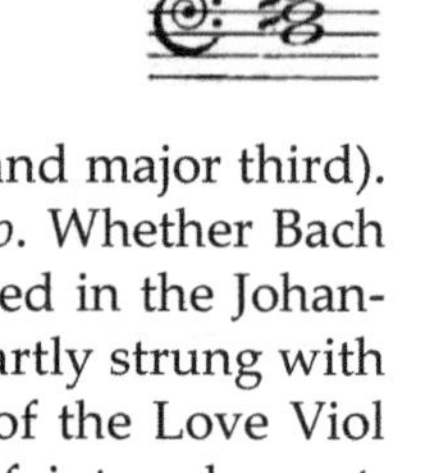

known as "Harp-way Sharp" (on account of the facile arpeggio and major third). This tuning was adopted by Meyerbeer for his graceful *obbligato*. Whether Bach wrote for a true viola d'amore is doubtful; the compass employed in the Johannis-Passion suggests an ordinary viola which might have been partly strung with steel or brass. Berlioz, in his *Treatise on Instrumentation*, writes of the Love Viol with sympathetic strings, "The quality of the Viole d'Amour is faint and sweet; there is something seraphic in its partaking at once of the viola and the harmonics of the violin. It is peculiarly suitable to the legato style, to dreamy melodies, and to the expression of æsthetic or religious feeling." It will, I think, be conceded that when an instrument which has gone out of fashion possesses some special quality, such as is found in this fascinating viol, there is sufficient justification for bringing it back into use.

The Viola d'Amore and other instruments in this work, that belong to the Music Class Room of Edinburgh University, have been drawn by permission of Professor Sir Herbert Oakeley, Mus. Doc., and composer to her Majesty the Queen for Scotland.

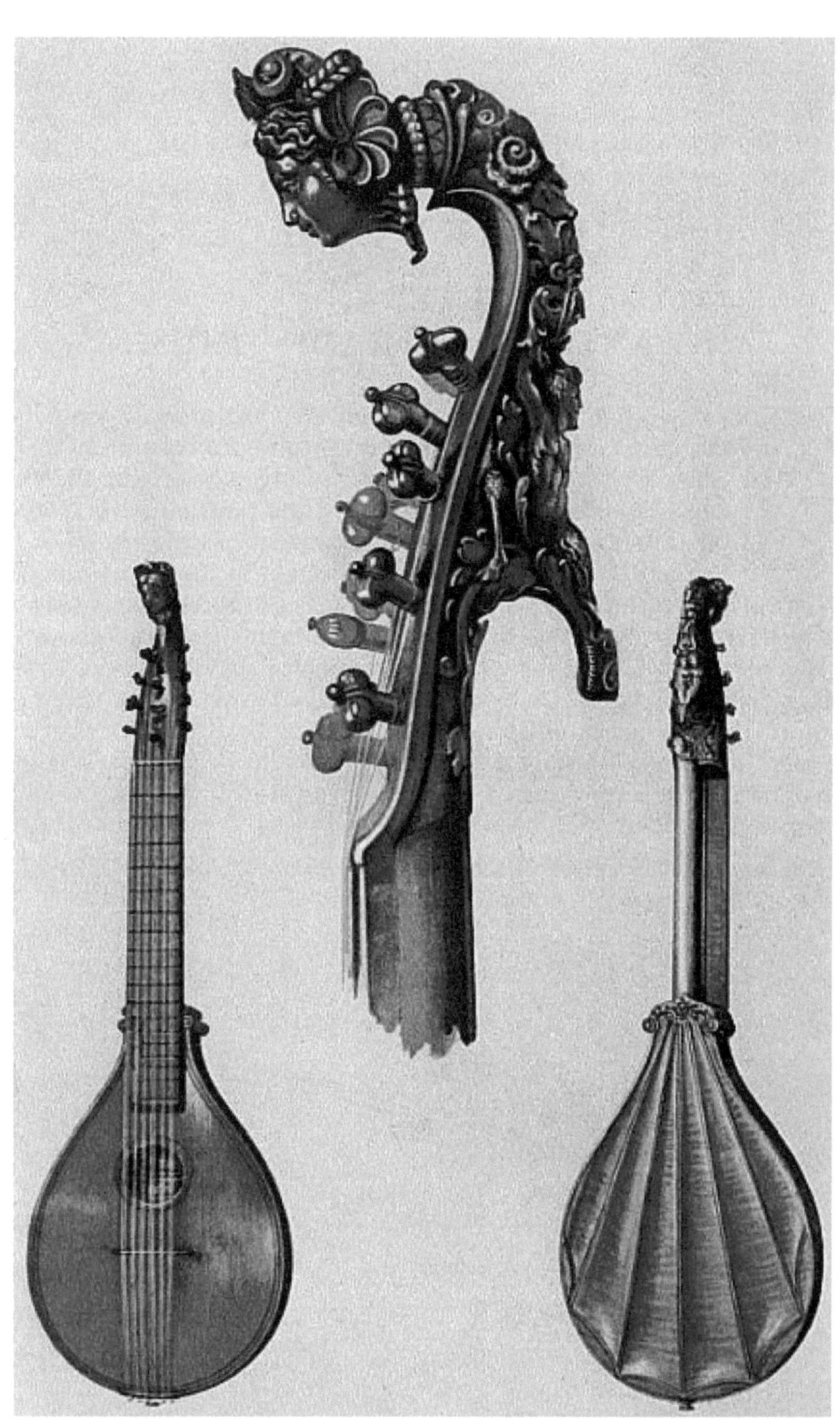

Plate XXVIII.

PLATE XXVIII.

CETERA, BY ANTONIUS STRADIVARIUS.

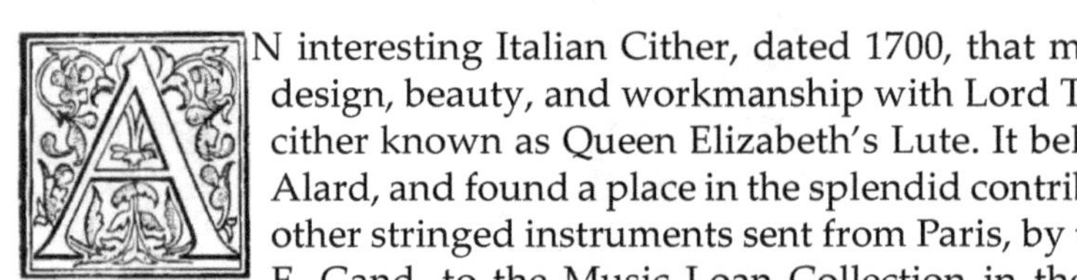

AN interesting Italian Cither, dated 1700, that may be compared for design, beauty, and workmanship with Lord Tollemache's English cither known as Queen Elizabeth's Lute. It belongs to the violinist Alard, and found a place in the splendid contribution of violins and other stringed instruments sent from Paris, by the mediation of Mr. E. Gand, to the Music Loan Collection in the Royal Albert Hall, 1885. It had also been lent by Mr. Vuillaume to the South Kensington Collection of 1872. This instrument, as well as the guitar drawn in the next Plate, show Stradivarius was not averse from making other instruments than violins. As well as cithers and guitars, he is known to have made a harp. Two views are given of this cetera, and one enlarged profile of the head and peg-box. It is a woman's head, said to represent Diana,—a satyr and nymph behind the peg-box serving to form a crook or handle for supporting the instrument, as the lizard in Mr. Donaldson's cetera already described.

It will be seen this Cetera differs from the Quinterna in Plate XXIII.; it is in form one of the oldest existing musical instruments.

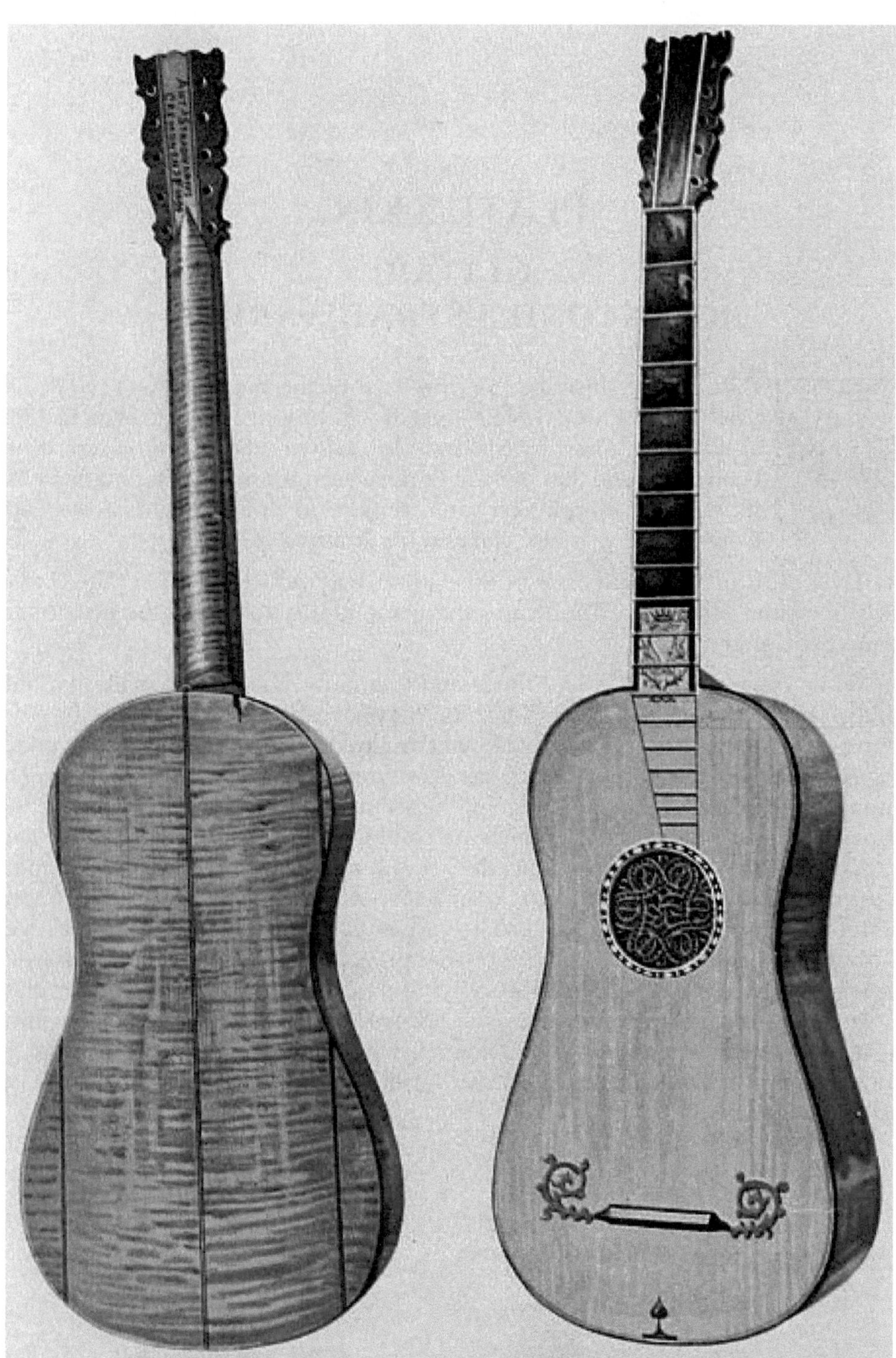

Plate XXIX.

PLATE XXIX.

GUITAR, BY ANTONIUS STRADIVARIUS.

THIS Guitar is inscribed on the back of the peg-box ANT^{S} STRADIVARIVS CREMONEN^{S}. F 1680. It was brought from Brescia in 1881, and was acquired by Messrs. W.E. Hill and Sons of London. It has been supposed that this might have been the only guitar made by the illustrious violin-maker; but another, in the Museum of the Paris Conservatoire, is also claimed for Stradivarius.

The beautiful arabesque rose of this Guitar will attract attention. The coat of arms upon the finger-board indicates the noble family to which the instrument formerly belonged.

While often made in Italy, France and Germany, the Guitar is the national Spanish instrument, and although fashion may for a time permit its use in other countries, it is as an exotic, for the character and traditions of the instrument attach it closely to Spain, where it is the universal accompaniment to song and dance. The Andalusian Seguidilla and Fandango with castanet accompaniment are characteristic measures for dances, with which are combined vocal performances of *coplas* and *estrevillo* (couplets of four short lines and a refrain of three), partaking more of the character of an improvisation than a set performance. In the north of Spain, the Jota Aragonesa and Jota Navarra are accompanied by a vocal refrain as well as castanets, hand-clapping and finger-snapping. All these Spanish dances are in triple time with certain peculiarities of rhythm; occasionally professed guitar players elaborate them into compositions of special interest and beauty, astonishing the listener with the capabilities of the Spanish guitar as a solo instrument. But, in truth, the artist will make himself felt, however limited the range and power of the instrument may be.

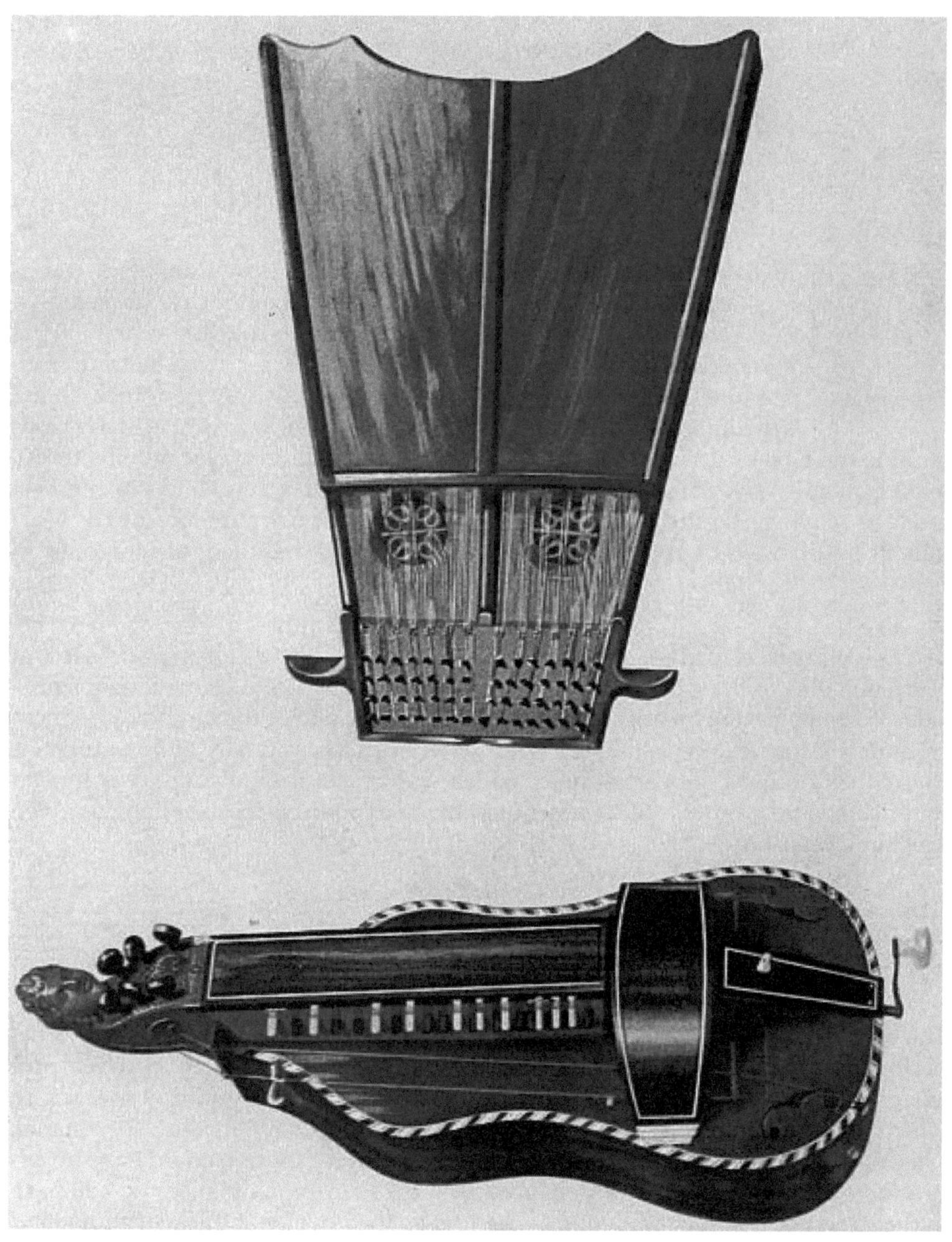

Plate XXX.

PLATE XXX.

BELL HARP AND HURDY-GURDY.

HE Bell Harp, although it appears in modern pre-Raphaelite paintings and is a kind of wire-strung psaltery, cannot be classed as a mediæval instrument, as it dates only from about the year 1700. Its invention is attributed to John Simcock, a soldier, who, judging from the label inside, probably gave the name of his superior officer to the instrument. It reads as follows:—"John Simcock, in the Right Honourable the Earl of Ancram's regiment of Dragoons, and in Captain Bell's troop, makes, mends, and sells the English harp; also instructs gentlemen in the best mode of playing that instrument." Robert, third Earl of Ancram, afterwards Marquis of Lothian, was appointed Colonel of the seventh regiment of Dragoons in 1696.

The Bell Harp here drawn belongs to Miss E.A. Willmott of Warley Place, Essex, as well as the Hurdy-Gurdy beneath it in the same Plate. It has four roses and fourteen notes of brass strings of four unisons to each. The extreme length of the sides is 21 inches; the breadth at the top is 6⅝ inches, and at the bottom, 13½ inches. Simcock constructed bell harps with more notes, occasionally of three unisons to each, excepting the deepest note, which was one string only, spun over with wire. The scale of another of sixteen notes, made by John Simcock at Bath, as given by Engel, was—

The bell harp, like the zither, is sounded with a plectrum on each thumb, and the performer, while twanging the strings rapidly, holds the harp by wooden projections from the sides of the frame, and swings it upwards and downwards, to which action Grassineau (*Musical Dictionary*, London, 1740) attributes the name. This may have been so, but it is certain that the swinging motion could have no appreciable effect upon the tone. A few years ago a Frenchman played the bell harp in the streets of London, attracting audiences by the novelty of the instrument and the grace with which he swung it.

THE HURDY-GURDY.

"With dead, dull, doleful, heavy hums,
With mournful moans, with grievous groans,
The sober hurdy-gurdy thrums."

These lines, from an Ode for St. Cecilia's Day, are said to have been set to music for ancient British instruments, by Arne. But they libel an instrument that has only failed from lack of inventors to attain to the development that has raised some of its former competitors to the consideration they are now held in. While the organistrum of the church became the vielle of the Jongleurs, passing into the chifonie and hurdy-gurdy of the common folk in the fifteenth and sixteenth centuries, the dulcimer has been the precursor of the pianoforte. The hurdy-gurdy, although at one time transformed to a sostenente key-board instrument described by Evelyn, and as the "Geigenwerk" exciting the attention of J.S. Bach, has remained what it was. The latest improved vielle or hurdy-gurdy had the following key-board compass and tuning of the open strings—

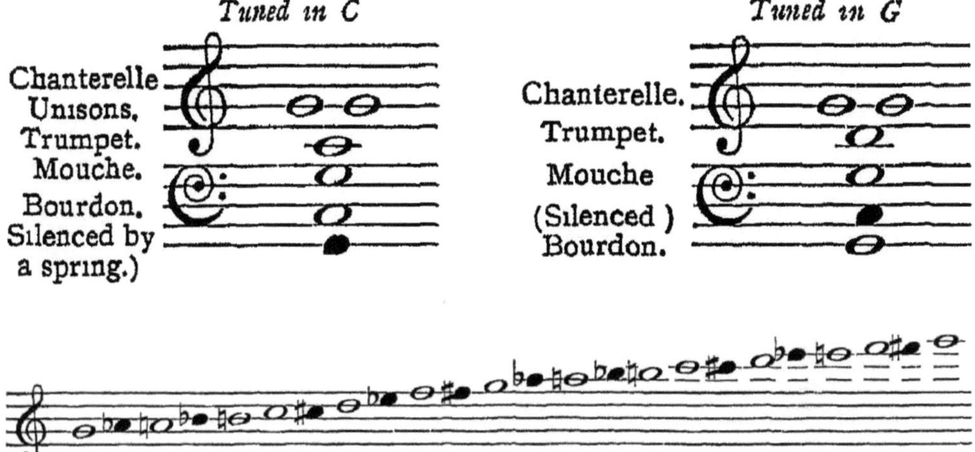

The open notes correspond with the long black keys of the instrument; the black notes with the short white keys.

The sound is produced by the vibration of the strings, maintained by the friction of a wheel with which they are brought into contact, the function of the rotary movement being analogous to that of the fiddler's bow, the wheel being also prepared, like the bow, with rosin. Sympathetic strings are not unfrequently attached.

The Hurdy-Gurdy here drawn has within the sound-body the maker's label, "Louvet, Luthier, à la Vielle Royale, rue de la Croix des Petits Champs, à la côté de la petite porte Saint Honoré à Paris, 1757." The length, without the head, is 19½ inches; the breadth being respectively 8⅛ and 10 inches across the belly at the wider measures. The carving of the head in this and many other vielles and viols is a message to us from the past of loving care bestowed.

Baton, a luthier of Versailles, introduced in the year 1716 improvements in the vielle, or hurdy-gurdy, one of which, by reducing it to the size of a guitar, made it more convenient for performance. He even went further by adapting it to lute and theorbo bodies, while he and his successors gradually extended the compass, the highest G being added by Louvet about 1773. It became for some time a fashionable instrument, and representations of the vielle and musette (a refined bagpipe) occur in contemporary French paintings. But after the French Revolution the hurdy-gurdy was relegated once more to the highways and byeways; the last popular street player in Paris was Barbu, who, according to Mr. Louis Pagnerre, was to be heard previous to 1870, in the Champs Elysées and other open spaces, and occasionally in the courtyards of the houses of his patrons. He sometimes gave concerts, for he was an artist, and had taste as well as executive talent; he could make the instrument sing, use it to accompany his own voice, or to take a part in combination with guitar and violin. He disdained to ask for money, relying upon the appreciation of his audiences to obtain his reward. Barbu had also been heard in London, and is supposed to have been shot during the Commune.

Plate XXXI.

PLATE XXXI.

SORDINI.

HE Sordino is a pocket fiddle, the "Pochette" of the French and the "Taschengeige" of the Germans. In form it is derived from the mediæval rebec which came from the East, and was also known as "gigue." It was distinguished from the viol family by the neck being a prolongation of the body of the instrument, instead of an attachment to it. A diminutive viol, the dancing master's kit, replaced the rebec kit, or sordino, at the beginning of the eighteenth century. A sordino, in the Museum of the Paris Conservatoire, with the date 1717, is believed to be unique as the undoubted work of Stradivarius. Tarisio, a well-known violin collector, brought it from Italy to France, and Louis Clapisson, the violinist, composer, and collector, eventually bought it in 1858, and employed it in his opera of "Les trois Nicolas," writing a gavotte for it. The late M. Chouquet (author of *Le Musée du Conservatoire National de Musique,* Paris, a catalogue *raisonné* of the musical instruments in that collection) has described, in enthusiastic terms, the effect of this little instrument when a gavotte was played upon it by Croisilles. "It was remembered," he says, "with pleasure by the old subscribers to the Opera Comique"—a remark that would seem to imply that the sordino, or pochette, had adequate power, and a special and agreeable quality of tone. The instrument is provided with four catgut strings, and *f* holes on either side the bridge. Two Sordini are represented in the three figures of this Plate, the one with a negro's head in two views, the other with a termination in ivory.

These Sordini belong to the Music Class Room, Edinburgh University.

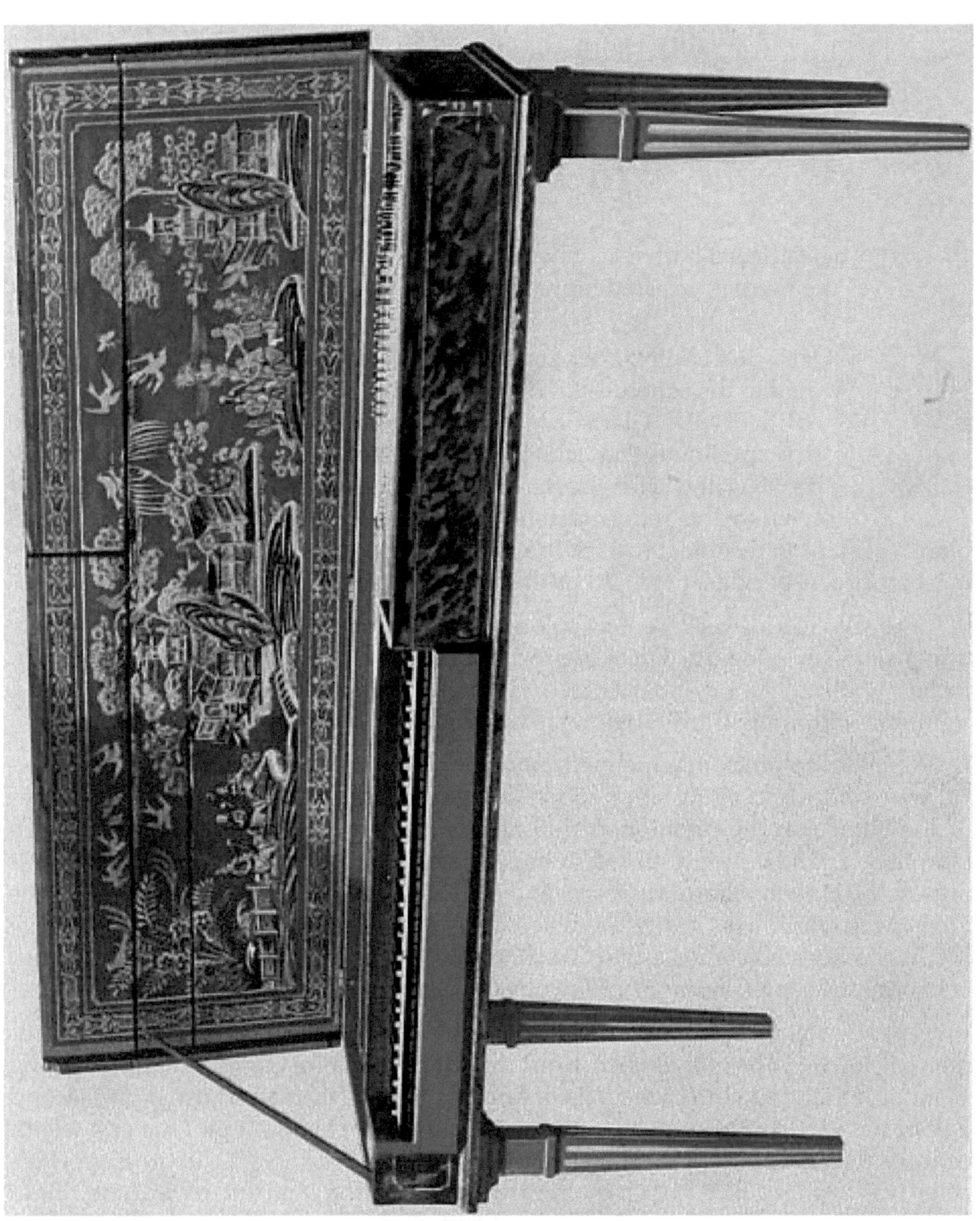

Plate XXXII.

PLATE XXXII.

CLAVICHORD.

"The claricord hath a tunely kynde
As the wyre is wrested high and lowe."

OHN SKELTON, Poet Laureate, who was born at Oxford in 1489, and died in the sanctuary, Westminster, in 1529, was the author of a poem entitled "The Claricorde," from which this quotation is taken. The true spelling is Clavichord, from the Latin "clavis," a key, and "chorda," a string. The wrester was the tuner, who wrested or strained the wire to the required tension. The words "wrest-pin" and "wrest-plank" remain in technical use for the tuning-pin and the wood in which the tuning-pins are inserted.

The Clavichord represented belongs to Mr. Gerald Wellesley, of London: its dimensions are—length, 5 feet 8½ inches; width, 1 foot 9 inches; and depth, 6½ inches; width of the key-board, 2 feet 9½ inches. The compass is five octaves and a semitone—from the third E below, to the third F above, middle C.

Chinese decoration, which was much in vogue in the early part of last century, was not unfrequently applied to clavichords and harpsichords. As examples of the latter may be mentioned the instrument that belonged to Queen Sophia Dorothea, until lately preserved in her palace at Charlottenburg, near Berlin, but now in the Hohenzollern Museum, and the Ruckers clavecin or harpsichord in the Turin Museum. There are two music parties or concerts shown within the lid of Mr. Wellesley's clavichord, with instruments that are not, however, Chinese, but conventional representations of European fiddles and guitars.

The Clavichord is, without question, the earliest key-board stringed instrument, it having been developed from the Monochord, used for teaching singing in monasteries and church schools. It appears to have come into use in the second half of the fourteenth century, but it was not until the beginning of the eighteenth century that it obtained its full development, when, in fact, its expressive character was brought into notice by improvements in the instrument and the finger technique. It was the Bachs who took advantage of this quality as the medium to express a characteristic and tender sentiment. Its gentle, intimate tone is produced by brass pins, called tangents, fixed in the keys and flattened at the upper ends. Raised to the strings in playing, these tangents set the strings in vibration, and at the same time form bridges to measure off the lengths required for the notes. The red cloth, woven in the strings behind the tangents, damps the sound. As far as we have met with the clavichords, the instrument has had two, sometimes three strings of brass wire to each note tuned in unison; the treble being, however, occasionally of steel wire to cause a brighter sound. There were sometimes octave strings to the lowest bass octave, after the manner of some theorboes, to make those notes distinct. These groups of unisons served for two, three, and even four notes according to the point of contact of the tangent affecting them, and to clavichords thus made the Germans applied the word "gebunden" (fretted). About the year 1700 each key obtained its own strings; and the instrument having become larger, it was more powerful and fitted to produce shades of sound of varying intensity. It had the "Bebung" as well, which is analogous to the violin-player's *vibrato*, and obtained by rocking the finger upon the key without quitting it. The clavichord is the only key-board instrument that allows this effect, but care has to be used to avoid an undue sharpening of the pitch of the note so treated—indeed, a constant equality of touch has to be maintained in playing the clavichord, to preserve an accurate intonation.

One of the most inspired compositions ever written for the clavichord is the "Fantasia Cromatica e Fuga," by Johann Sebastian Bach. The figuration, the manner of slurring, the arpeggios, and much more in this piece, are extremely characteristic of the instrument. For a performance intended to reproduce, as far as may be possible, the original reading, the piece should be first studied upon a clavichord, not a pianoforte. The gentle influence of the instrument soon makes itself felt, and both player and listener seem to breathe another and a purer atmosphere. But such a performance demands concentration and those quiet surroundings the old composers enjoyed.

I'm never merry when I hear sweet music;
The reason is your spirits are attentive.

SHAKSPEARE.

Music, which gentlier on the spirit lies,
Than tired eyelids upon tired eyes.

TENNYSON.

Plate XXXIII.

PLATE XXXIII.

THE EMPRESS HARPSICHORD.

EPRESENTS a Harpsichord of the largest size, the culmination of an instrument that had remained in use for nearly three hundred years, but, at the time this one was made, was about to be replaced by the pianoforte. This fine Harpsichord bears the joint names of Shudi and Broadwood, and was made at the house now known as No. 33 Great Pulteney Street, London, where the pianoforte business of Messrs. John Broadwood and Sons is still carried on. The instrument is numbered 691, and the books of the original firm show that it was made for the Empress Maria Theresa, and shipped on the 20th of August 1773, which happened to be the day after Shudi died. But he had for some time retired from harpsichord-making, and this instrument is really to be attributed to his son-in-law, John Broadwood. Burkhard Tschudi, or Shudi as he wrote his name in England, was of a noble Swiss family. He had established his business as a harpsichord-maker, in Great Pulteney Street, about 1732. Through Handel's friendship he became patronised by Frederick, Prince of Wales, father of George III., and was permitted to use the sign of "The Plume of Feathers" for his house. He was honoured with a commission from Maria Theresa's old enemy, Frederick the Great, to make two harpsichords for the "Neues Palais" at Potsdam, where they are still to be seen. One of them is described, with Silbermann's Forte Piano, in Dr. Burney's famous tour. Some years previously, Shudi had made a harpsichord and presented it to Frederick on the occasion of his victory at Prague, but the present writer could not find the instrument when he made a special visit to Berlin and Potsdam, in 1881. It may be said of Shudi and Jacob Kirkman, once fellow-apprentices, and afterwards competitors, that they left the harpsichord a more powerful instrument, and more varied in effect, by means of stops and registers, than it had ever been before.

Shudi was the inventor of the Venetian Swell (patented 1769), which he intended for the harpsichord. When the patent expired this contrivance was generally adopted in England, and becoming transferred to the organ, has remained, ever since, an important means of effect in that instrument. The figure in the Plate shows the Venetian Swell open, as it would be when the right pedal is put down. There are four registers and six stops in this instrument. Taking them in their order from left to right, we find on the left-hand side, the "lute," the jacks or plectra of which twang the first unison string, near the wrest-plank bridge, and give a more reedy sound than is obtained from the usual striking-places; the "octave," which, as its name indicates, acts upon strings tuned an octave higher, which are of shorter length, and lie below the others; and the "buff" (sometimes called "harp") stop, which partly mutes the second unison strings, throughout, by the contact of small pads of leather. On the right-hand side are the first and second rows of unison strings. The upper key-board has the first unison and lute only, while all the registers come under the player's control on the lower key-board. The machine stop, at the left hand of the key-boards, permits an agreeable change to lute and buff (harp) by using the left pedal and both sets of keys. Kirkman appears to have arranged his left-hand stops differently—buff, lute, octave. The dimensions of the Harpsichord here drawn are 8 feet 9¾ inches in extreme length, and 3 feet 4 inches in width at the key-boards. The great width of the key-board of the modern pianoforte renders it impossible, in designing one, to reproduce the special grace of the harpsichord.

Among composers, those who have best understood the genius of the harpsichord have been Handel and Scarlatti. The former, with his famous Air with variations in D Minor and the Presto following it, summed up the history and technique of the instrument, as far as it was then known. Scarlatti found such new features to display in technical contrivance and effect, that we are still attracted by an individuality the originality of which is, as yet, untouched by time. The only parallel instance, although resembling it in no other way, is that of Frédéric Chopin as a composer and performer on the pianoforte.

With the harpsichord went out the figured bass accompaniment, or thorough bass, that, for two hundred years, had been the foundation of a correct musical education. By degrees the training for technique and memory came to occupy that attention with pianoforte-players, which had been devoted to developing the fluency of improvisation expected from the harpsichord-player.

This harpsichord was lent by Mr. Victor Mahillon, of Brussels, to the South Kensington Music Loan Collection, 1885.

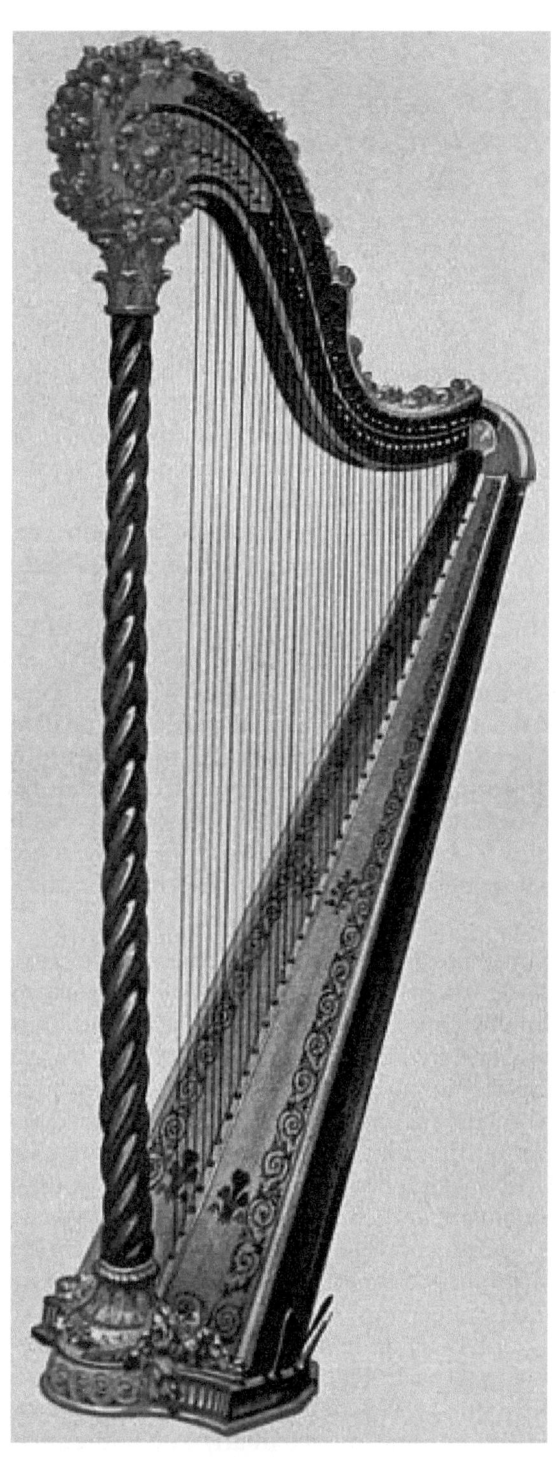

Plate XXXIV.

PLATE XXXIV.

PEDAL HARP.

GREEN and gold Harp that once belonged to George IV., and is now in the possession of Mr. Edward Joseph, of London. It is 5 feet 3 inches high, 2 feet 6 inches in extreme width, and 1 foot 9 inches wide at the base. It was included in the characteristic Louis Seize Historic Room, in the Music Loan Collection, Royal Albert Hall, 1885. This room, one of three, was so contrived as to display the musical instruments in social use with such surroundings of furniture, paintings, etc., as would be true for the period. These Historic Rooms, suggested by Mr. Alfred Maskell, the official superintendent of the Music Loan Collection, were arranged with great knowledge and taste by Mr. George Donaldson. They represented an English apartment of the time of George I., a Tudor apartment that included Queen Elizabeth's virginal, and a Louis Seize apartment that, with the Harp in the accompanying Plate, contained also the beautifully painted Ruckers clavecin or harpsichord (lent by Viscount Powerscourt) that had belonged to the unfortunate Marie Antoinette. There is a photograph of this harpsichord in the Catalogue of the South Kensington Collection, 1872, and a wood engraving of the Louis Seize room, showing both harpsichord and harp, in the *Art Journal* for August 1885.

The first pedal mechanism was invented by Hochbrucker, a Bavarian, about 1720; by it he rendered the harp fit for changes of key, possible before, and that only partially, by clumsy contrivances. By using a pedal to raise each open string a semitone, accomplished by pressure upon the strings, he gave the harp eight major and five complete minor scales—also three descending minor. The Cousineaus, who were Frenchmen, and father and son, superseded the contrivance of Hochbrucker by another that grasped or pinched the strings with pieces of metal on either side, and also by slides raising or lowering the bridge-pins. By doubling the pedals and mechanism, and changing the key of the open strings from E♭ to C♭, they, about 1782, produced the first double-action harp. It was, however, left for Sebastian Erard to perfect the harp by means of a fork mechanism of most ingenious contrivance. He began with the single-action harp about 1786, turning his attention to the double-action in 1801. It was not, however, until 1810 that he succeeded in producing the culmination of his various improvements in a harp of great beauty of tone, with seven pedals and two transpositions, the semitone and the whole tone, permitting performance in any key without change of fingering. In spite of these important inventions the harp has almost lost position as a solo instrument. It has, however, been taken advantage of by modern composers, who have adopted it, with charming effect, as an orchestral instrument.

Plate XXXV.

PLATE XXXV.

STATE TRUMPET AND KETTLEDRUM.

HIS silver state trumpet, with nine others, adorned with bannerets of the Royal Arms in crimson and gold, and silver state kettledrums, similarly adorned, belong to the collection of H.M. the Queen, in St. James's Palace. They were both probably made in the reign of George III., one of the trumpets in the collection bearing the maker's name, William Shaw, Red Lion Street, Holborn. Henry VIII. had fourteen trumpets in his Royal Band, while Queen Elizabeth, in 1587, had ten.

The bending back of the trumpet upon itself, now a well-known feature in the appearance of the instrument, was an invention of a Frenchman towards the end of the fifteenth century. The trumpet is one of the oldest wind instruments used in concert with others. As far back as 1607 a piece for five trumpets, in the *Orfeo* of Monteverde, was played at the Court of Mantua. It became an instrument much cultivated, and Handel's and Bach's parts for it are of extreme difficulty. The notes of the trumpet are the natural harmonics produced by varying pressure of the lips in the mouthpiece. Recently slides and pistons have been employed to augment its compass, and render its employment easier.

The State Trumpets were sounded to announce the arrival of Her Majesty the Queen at Westminster Abbey on the occasion of the Thanksgiving Service for her Jubilee on the 21st of June, 1887, as they had been on the 20th of the same month, fifty years before, to proclaim her Accession. The Fanfare for four trumpets played at the Jubilee Service by the State Trumpeters is here given by the kind permission of the composer, Mr. Thomas Harper, a famous player himself upon the slide trumpet, an instrument now not much known on the Continent.

The State Kettledrum of silver and draped with the Royal banner, represents the only member of the Drum family capable of being tuned to the pitch of the band with a clearly recognisable note. The head is of vellum stretched upon a ring fitting closely round the kettle of the drum. Screws, working on this ring, tighten or slacken the head to produce the note required from its compass. The pair of kettledrums are usually tuned to tonic and dominant, but inequalities of tension in the head, owing to the membrane not being perfectly homogeneous, interfere with the notes being strictly accurate.

1st
2nd
3rd
4th
Trumpets
in D.

3
3
3
3
3
3
3
3

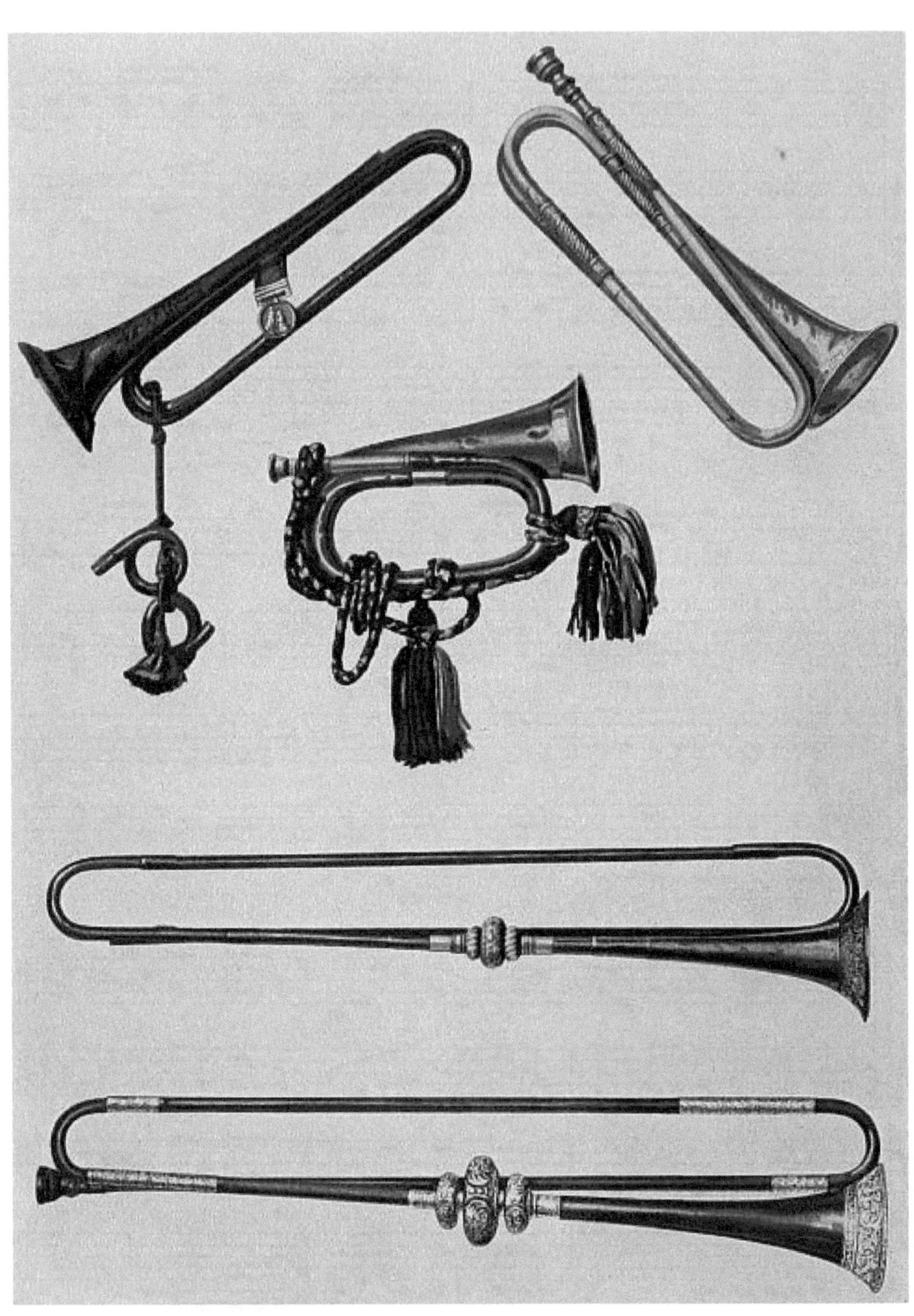

Plate XXXVI.

PLATE XXXVI.

CAVALRY BUGLE, WITH TASSELS.
CAVALRY TRUMPET, EMBOSSED.
TRUMPETS, THREE INSTRUMENTS— WITH CROOKS, GILT, AND SILVER MOUNTED.

HE Cavalry Bugle, decorated with tassels and graciously contributed by H.R.H. the Prince of Wales, President of the International Inventions Exhibition, 1885, to the Music Loan Collection, has an historical interest in having been used by Trumpeter Smith to sound the moonlight charge of the Household Cavalry and 7th Dragoon Guards, at Kassassin in Egypt, August the 28th, 1882.

The Trumpet with crooks was carried by Sergeant-Major Webb of the 5th Dragoon Guards, Field Trumpeter to the Duke of Wellington, and with this instrument he sounded the grand charge at the Battle of Salamanca, July the 22nd, 1812. It is the property of a descendant of the Sergeant-Major, Mr. Joseph Webb, who contributes the veteran's description, often repeated to him, of the anxious moment when the command was given to sound the charge. "I trembled all over as I lifted the trumpet to my mouth, for I could see what the boys had before them, but as soon as my lips touched the mouthpiece fear left me, and I blew such a charge as I never had before or could afterwards."

The embossed Cavalry Trumpet, with a very heavy mouthpiece, belonging to Mr. A.W. Malcolmson, is English, and was made by William Sandbach in the last century. The remaining trumpets belong to Mr. Thomas Harper, the gilt one having been made by John Harris about 1730, and the silver-mounted one by William Bull about 1680.

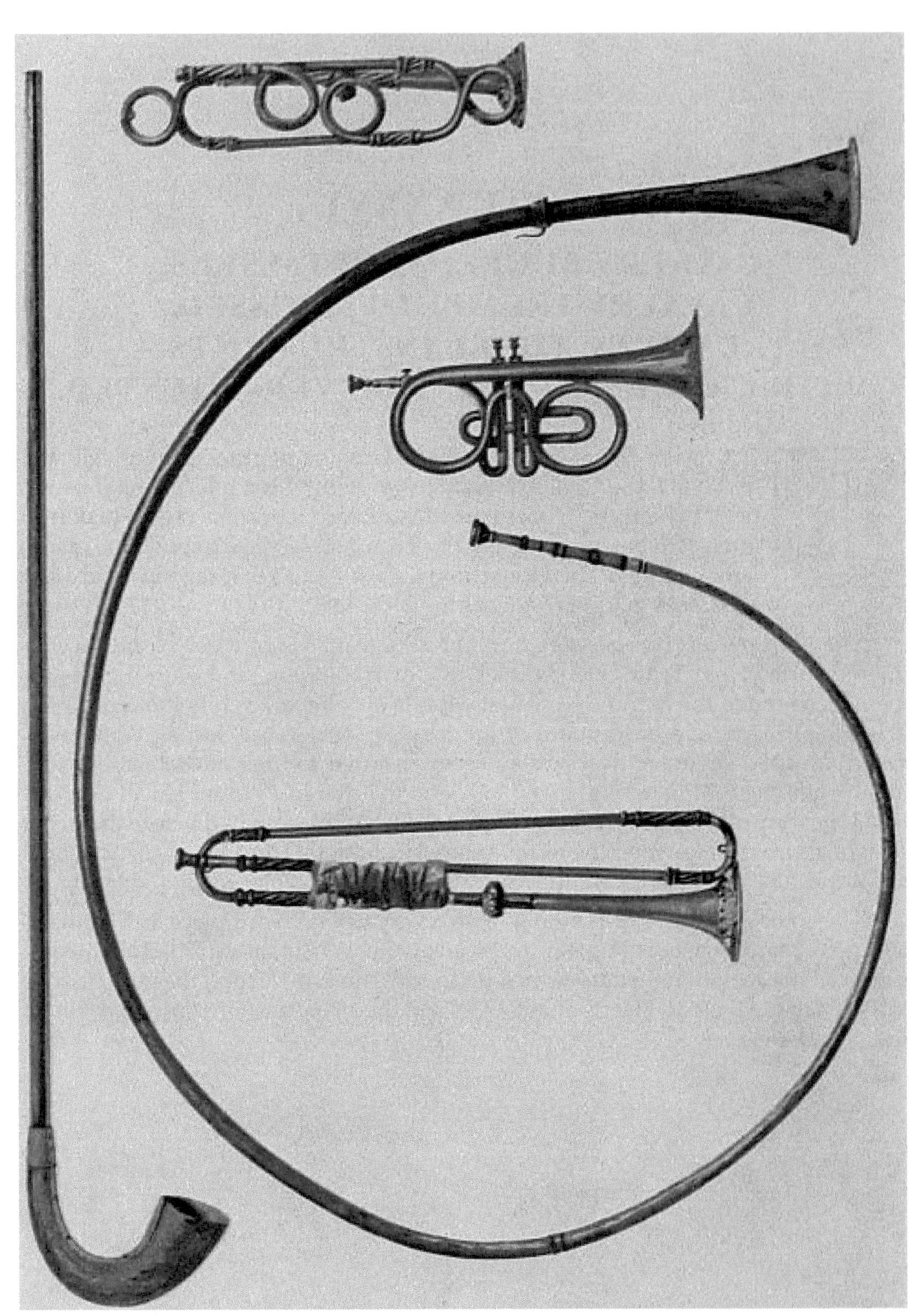

Plate XXXVII.

PLATE XXXVII.

LITUUS, ROMAN CAVALRY. BUCCINA, ROMAN INFANTRY. CORNET, WITH TWO VALVES. TRUMPETS.

HE Roman Lituus, the antique straight instrument with the curved end, is drawn from a reproduction in bronze of the original, found in the tomb of a warrior discovered in 1827, at Cervetri, the Etruscan Caere, and preserved in the Museum of the Vatican. The lituus took its name from the augur's staff, which it resembled in shape; it belonged to the cavalry of the Roman Empire. It produces the following proper notes or natural harmonics—

the seventh being flatter than the note which occurs in our modern musical scale. The fundamental 1 which the length of this tube—5 feet 4 inches—would give, cannot be produced. It was from a minute description of the original instrument, by Signor Alessandro Kraus junior of Florence, that Mr. Victor Mahillon was enabled to make this interesting reproduction of an instrument which appears to be the only antique trumpet known. The curved Buccina is from another reproduction by him of an instrument preserved in the Museum at Naples, and found in excavating Pompeii. It was passed under the left arm of the executant and over his right shoulder, in a manner easily adopted by a foot-soldier. This Buccina is in unison with the horn in G, and has a bugle quality of tone. Its notes are—

the seventh and eleventh harmonics not being in tune with the corresponding notes in our received scales, and the fundamental being again impracticable. To sound the lituus and buccina is to awaken the echoes of the ancient past; but, whether blown by Roman or Greek or Egyptian, we may be sure the harmonic division of a column of air into vibrating sections knows no change, and was the same then as now.

The Cornet with two valves shows one of the earliest adaptations of the now dominant pistons as introduced by C. Saxe of Brussels.

One Trumpet, by Johann Wilhelm Haas of Nuremberg, is of obsolete make; the other, also by Haas, is curved in half-circles to facilitate the production of stopped notes, and is curiously engraved.

These five instruments belong to the Brussels Conservatoire Royal.

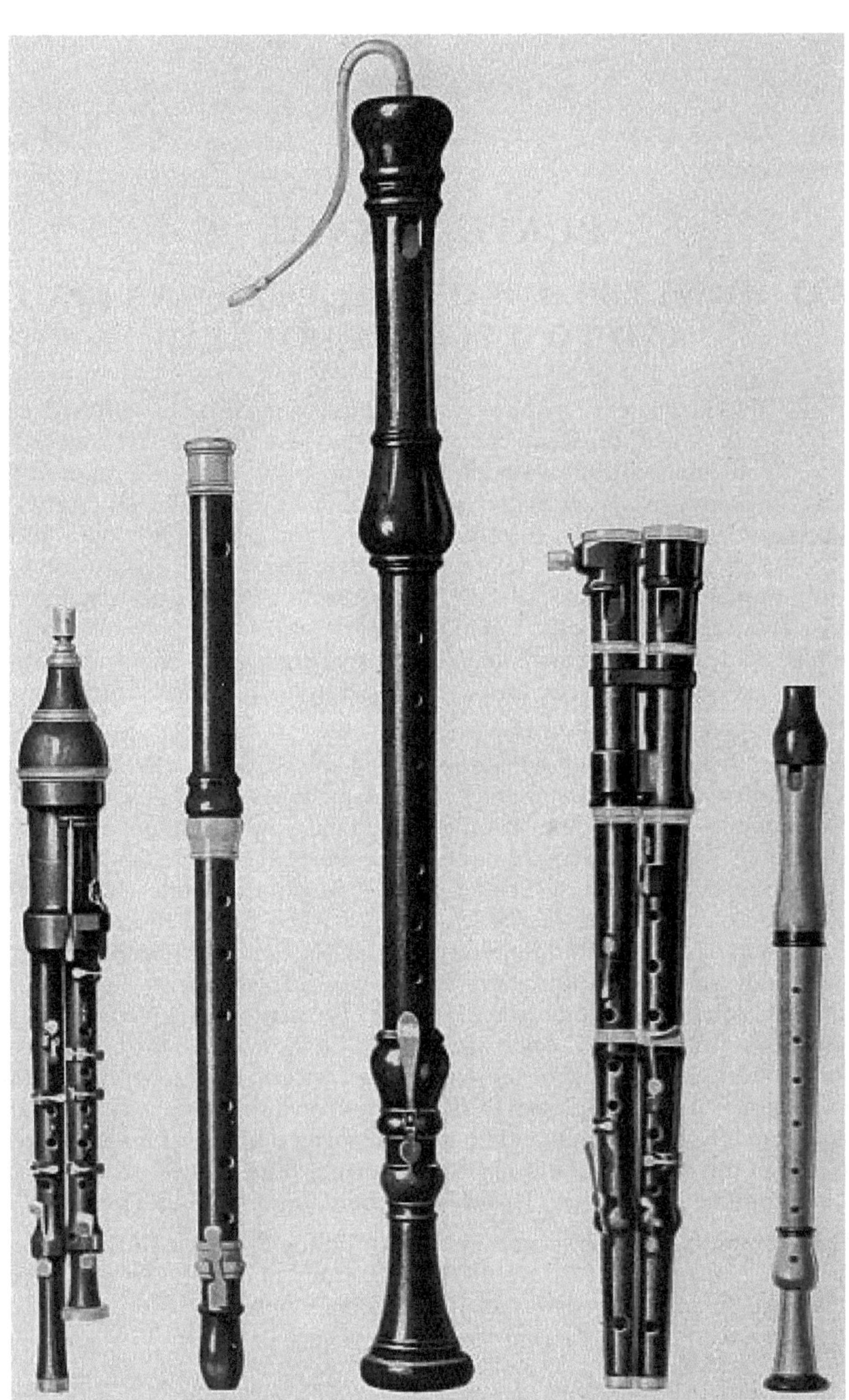

Plate XXXVIII.

PLATE XXXVIII.

TWO DOUBLE FLAGEOLETS, A GERMAN FLUTE, AND TWO FLÛTES DOUCES.

HE Flageolet is the last example in present use of the "flûtes douces," or "à bec" (German Blockflöten), bored with reversed cones, that is to say, with the embouchure at the larger end. It is referred to by Pepys in his *Diary* (1st March, 1666): "Being returned home I find Greeting, the flageolet-master, come, and teaching my wife, and I do think my wife will take pleasure in it, and it will be easy for her, and pleasant;" and again (20th January, 1667): "To Drumbleby's the pipe-maker, there to advise about the making of a flageolet to go low and soft; and he do show me a way which do do, and also a fashion of having two pipes of the same note fastened together, so as I can play in one and then echo it upon the other, which is mighty pretty."

The double flageolets in the Plate were made by W. Bainbridge, London, who had a speciality for such instruments. The flûtes douces—in Shakspeare's *Hamlet* the "Recorders"—were made in families like viols, cromornes, shawms, and other well-known Elizabethan instruments, a fashion that modern instrumentation shows a tendency to return to. Evelyn, in 1679, mentions them as "now in much request for accompanying the voice." A bass and treble flute is drawn, also a one-keyed German or transverse flute which, in the last century, from its beauty and tone, although defective in intonation, was a favourite instrument, and supplanted the flûte douce in public favour. In the concerts of ancient music given in July, 1885, by members of the Brussels Conservatoire in the Music Room of the Inventions Exhibition, South Kensington, a movement from a Concerto by Quanz (music-master to Frederick the Great) was played by Mr. Dumon on a single-keyed ivory flute. In the same concerts, Mr. Dumon and his pupils played a March of the Lansquenets, of the time of the Peace of Cambrai (1519), on eight flûtes douces (flauti dolci), in parts, accompanied by a drum. This was the military music of that period.

The German flute is the second instrument in the Plate; the flûtes douces are the third and fifth from left to right. These instruments and those drawn in the next Plate are the property of Messrs. J. & R. Glen, Edinburgh.

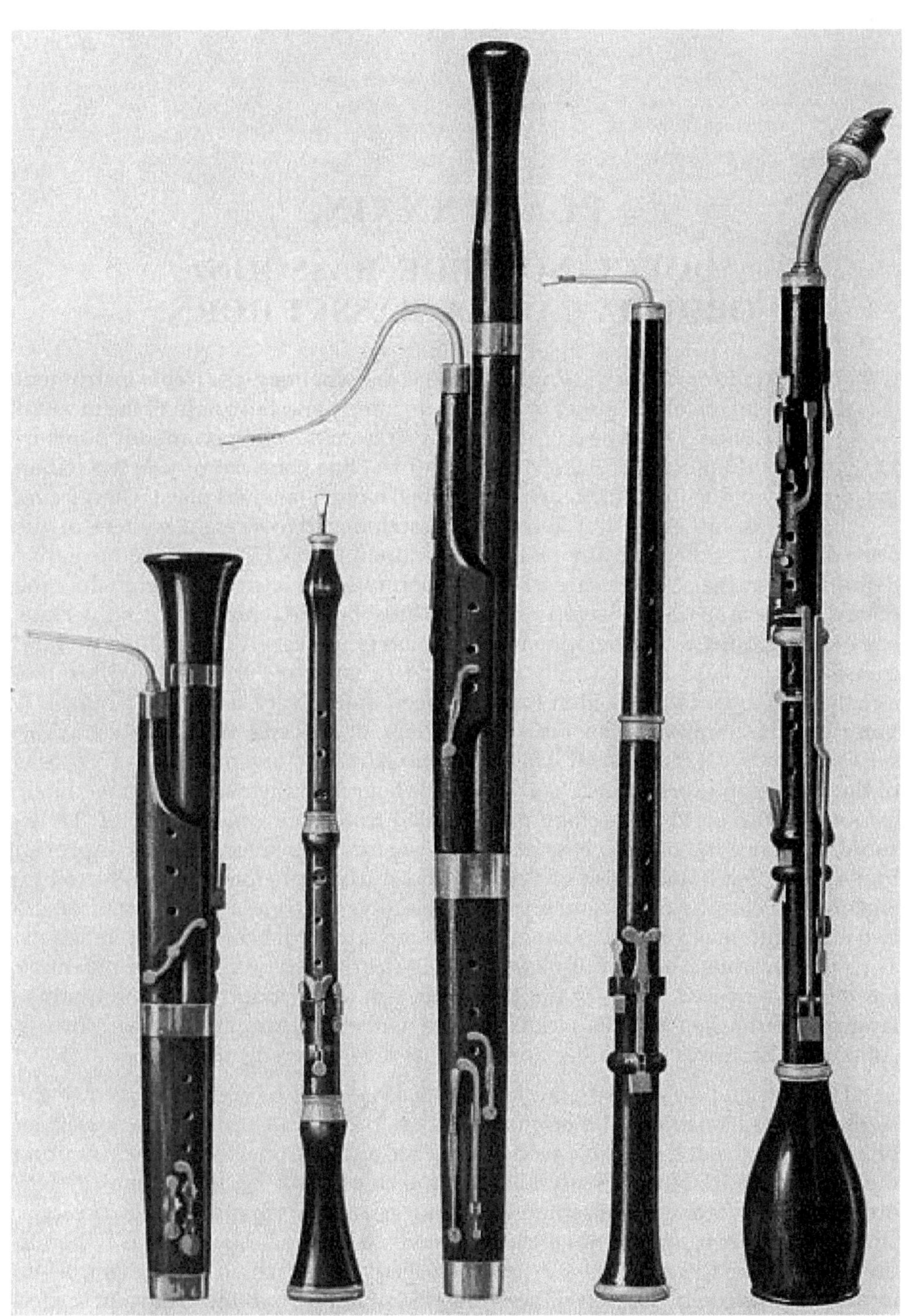

Plate XXXIX.

PLATE XXXIX.

DOLCIANO. OBOE. BASSOON. OBOE DA CACCIA. BASSET HORN.

HE shawm of the English Bible is the schalmey, the treble instrument of the old Pommer or Bombardo family and the origin of the modern oboe. The oboe da caccia, derived from the alto pommer or Bombardo piccolo of the sixteenth century, has gone out of use, the Italian corno inglese (French cor anglais) having taken its place. There being some confusion about the description by different writers of the oboe da caccia and oboe d'amore, I fall back upon Dr. W.H. Stone's authoritative definition that the oboe da caccia is a bassoon raised a fourth in pitch, while the oboe d'amore is an oboe lowered a fifth. The bassoon, the centre figure in the Plate, has been regarded as a development of the bass pommer or Bombardone, and the transformation has been generally attributed to a canon of Ferrara named Afranio, a native of Pavia. This question has now been definitively settled by Count L.F. Valdrighi, the librarian of the Biblioteca Estense at Modena. He has proved (*Musurgiana,* No. 5, "Il Phagotus d'Afranio"), that Afranio's invention, *ante* 1539, was of the nature of a corna musa (cornemuse or bagpipe), the bag being most likely combined with soft bass melody pipes, called from their quality of tone "Dolcisuoni," whence the dolcino bass of church organs. This invention was improved by Giambattista Ravilio, also of Ferrara, and thirty years later was perfected by Sigismund Scheltzer of Nuremberg, who, rejecting the cornemuse bag, united the two tubes into the "fagotto," so named from the fascine of beech (fagus), or fagots. The fagotto is the same as our bassoon. This clearing up of a disputed invention has been discovered in a very unlikely place—in an Introduction to the Chaldee language, published in 1539, written by the nephew of Afranio, Teseo-Ambrogio Albonesio, Professor of Chaldee and Syriac at the University of Bologna.

The dolciano, to the extreme left of the Plate, will be thus seen to owe the suggestion of its name to the original bassoon. But this instrument has a clarinet or beating reed, not the double reed of the oboe and bassoon. I state this fact upon the high authority of Mr. Henry Lazarus, the clarinet-player, who names it "tenoroon," but Dr. Stone has accepted this name as a synonym of the oboe da caccia, and calls this instrument with a clarinet reed, "dolciano." Mr. Lazarus, when in the Band of the Royal Military Asylum, played upon such an instrument, as he informs me, made by Garrett of Westminster, at a date that must have preceded Sax's invention, which combined the conical tube and clarinet reed in the Saxophone. The basset horn, or corno di bassetto, to the extreme right of the Plate, is the alto clarinet, a fifth lower in pitch than the clarinet in C. It is said to have been invented at Passau in Bavaria in 1770, but the name of the inventor is not recorded. It was improved by Lotz of Presburg in 1782, and again by Iwan Müller in 1812. Mozart wrote two parts for basset horns in his famous Requiem. The relative positions in the Plate of the Oboe and Oboe da Caccia are indicated above.

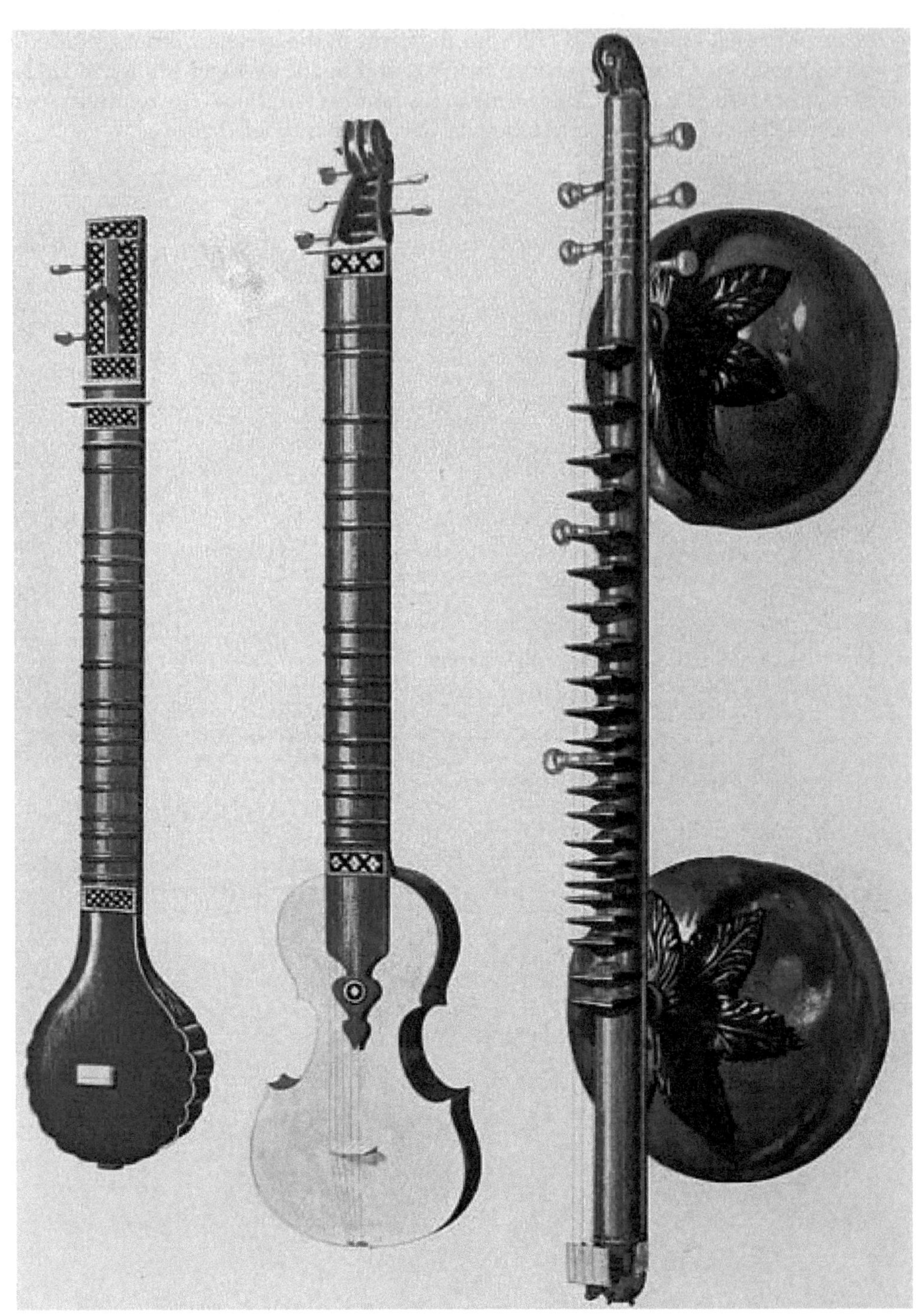

Plate XL.

PLATE XL.

SITÁRS AND VÍNA.

HE Sitár is the favourite instrument of Upper India, and was reintroduced and perfected by the poet-musician Amir Khusru of Delhi in the thirteenth century. The name is Persian, and implies "three strings," although the Sitár has now usually five, six, and sometimes seven strings. Sitárs called *Taruffe* have sympathetic strings of fine wire attached to the side of the neck and passing underneath the frets and bridge, to vibrate in unison with the notes of the same pitch that are played. This contrivance, although of recent date in Europe, is of great antiquity in the East, being mentioned in the Sangíta Ratnâkera, the earliest known work in Sanscrit upon music. The principal strings of the Sitár are sounded by a wire plectrum worn upon the forefinger of the player's right hand; and their accordance, which was noted when given to Mr. A.J. Ellis and myself by H.H. The Rájah Rám Pál Singh, an Indian prince residing in England, who played upon a fine Sitár now in my possession, is  . Here the keynote, or khuruj, is F. This method of tuning, although not so common as tunings given later, is employed in the north of India and the Punjab; and a similar employment of the second and third for open strings may be found in the tuning of the Surs'ringâra. The F string is the melody string stopped by the frets. The other strings are occasionally struck, but are rarely fretted, and never to produce harmony. The brass frets are secured to the neck by catgut ties, and are movable, so that by changing their positions different modes are obtained. The classical Sanscrit name for the Sitár, the instrument drawn on the left, was Tritantri (three-stringed) Vína. A form of Sitár, with a flat body, was called Káchapi (Kacchapa, a tortoise) Vína, now known as Káchwâ Sitár. The usual tuning of Sitárs having from three to seven strings is to these intervals:—

In these tunings C is the khuruj or keynote, the melody string being máhdyamâ or F. Sitárs have usually seventeen to eighteen frets. The five methods of arranging them, so as to produce different modes, styled Thât, are as follows:—

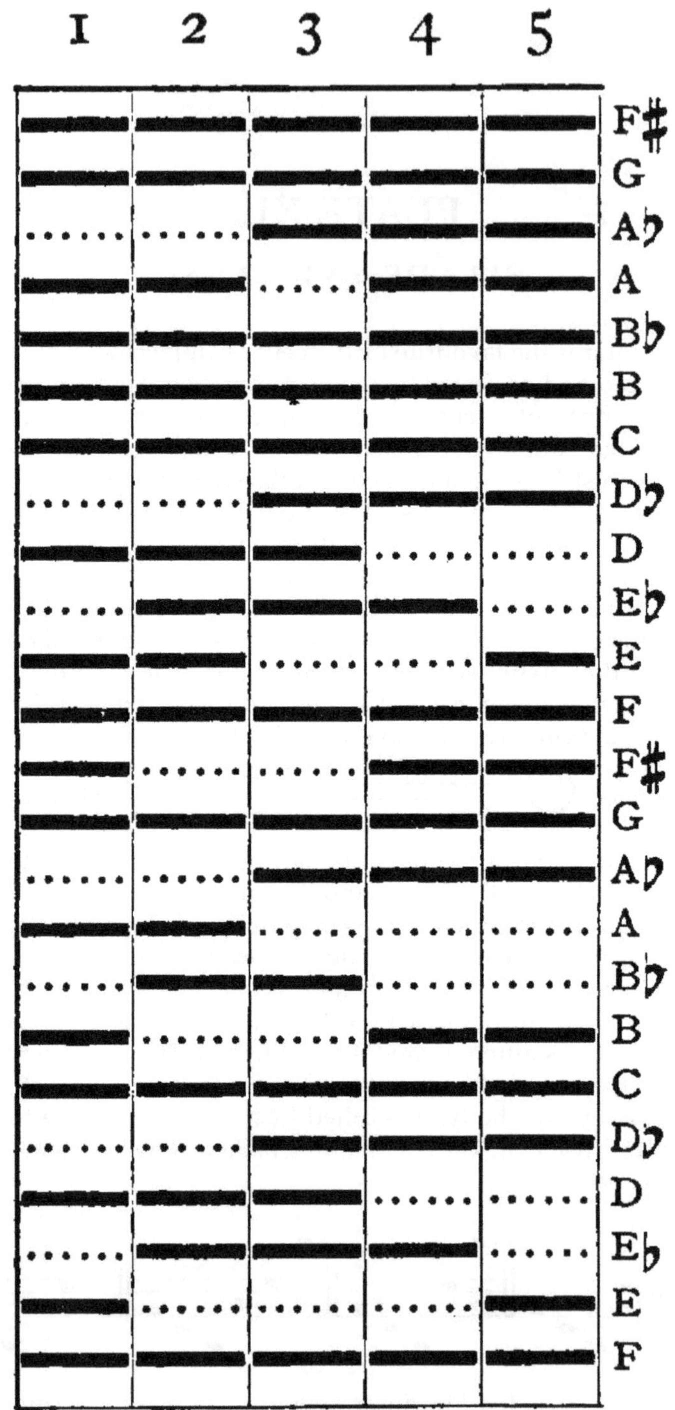

Intervals upon the F or melody string.

The word "Thât," employed to signify scale or mode, should not be confounded with "Râga," the foundation of all Indian music. Râga has no equivalent in European musical language, but may be described as a melody type founded upon the intervals of a mode, and having a succession of notes so arranged as to excite a certain feeling of the mind. There may be many melodies in the same râga, differing distinctly from each other. Methods for the Sitár have been written in Bengâli by the Rájah Sir S.M. Tagore, a well-known amateur, and in Mahrátti by a Brahmin musician of Poona, Anna Ghárpure, a fine performer now in the service of H.H. the Thâkore Sahib of Wadhwân. Besides the Rájah Rám Pál Singh, I had an opportunity of hearing a player from Jeypur, at an exhibition called "India in London," in 1886. The technique and charm of his performance are not easily forgotten. The resonance body of an ordinary Sitár is a gourd, but he had one with two gourds, known as the "Been," or Vína Sitár.

The Sitár in the centre, with fiddle-shaped body, is the Súrsanga, or Esrar without sympathetic strings, a bowed instrument combining the Sitár with the Sárungí. It is a modern instrument, and is intended to accompany women's voices. It has four strings, tuned, upon the authority of the Rájah Sir S.M. Tagore, as given by Mr. Victor Mahillon in his admirable Catalogue of the Museum of the Brussels Conservatoire, .

The third instrument, upon the right, attached to two gourds, is the Mahati or great Vína—known now as the "Been." It is the most ancient and finest Indian instrument, and is also the most difficult to play. It is composed of a bamboo resting upon two gourds, and has seven strings—two at the side nearest the F or melody string, four over the frets, and one at the side away from the melody string. The tuning, the pitch varying with the size of the instrument, is as follows:—

The string × is tuned E or A as required in the "râga" played. In the drawing five strings have been shown over the frets; the string, however, from the peg above and nearest to the nut, should pass over a small ivory head, not shown, but placed on the side of the bamboo, between the second and third frets, to the small bridge shown at the farthest end of the instrument at the side, and not over the main bridge. The frets, twenty-two in number, are at semitonic intervals, and fixed. The instrument is played with two plectra upon the first two fingers of the player's right hand; the two side strings are struck by the nail of the little finger moved upwards; the single side string, upon the other side, is struck by the little finger of the left hand when required. The instrument is held with the gourd nearest the nut resting upon the left shoulder, while the right gourd rests beneath the right arm. It should be noted that the disposition of strings is, in Vínas, reversed from that of Sitárs. There is a peculiarly soft and plaintive quality of tone in the Vína that is altogether wanting in the Sitár.

There are two systems of music in vogue in India at the present day—the Karnâtik or southern system, and the Hindustâni or northern. The latter is chiefly in the hands of Mahomedan professors, who have borrowed from the Arabian and Persian systems. The Karnâtik is more melodious, and possesses fewer traces of foreign innovation. Instruments used by Karnâtik professors employ only the intervals of the tonic fourth and fifth (or their octaves) upon the open strings. Hence we find the southern Indian Vína—an instrument with only one resonance gourd, and a wooden body like a lute—tuned to the following intervals:—

or

the first method being known as "Pánchamâ s'ruti," the latter as "Máhdyamâ s'ruti," from the relative intervals between the strings.

The illustrations of the Súrsanga, Mahati Vína, and three-stringed Sitár, are from a fine Indian collection, divided by the Rájah Sir Sourindro Mohun Tagore between the Brussels Conservatoire and the London Royal College of Music.

For completing this information concerning Indian stringed instruments, as well as that of the Indian Drums in Plate XLI., I am indebted to one of the highest authorities on the subject, Lieutenant C.R. Day, Oxfordshire Light Infantry (late 43rd), whose recent personal experience and searching studies have been generously placed by him at my disposal.

Plate XLI.

PLATE XLI.

INDIAN DRUMS.

AINTED instruments consisting of a wooden drum, one of earthenware, and a Tam-Tam. The employment of such instruments is necessarily rhythmic, and they occupy a place on the borderland of music and mere noise. Mr. Rowbotham, however (*History of Music*, vol. i., London, 1885), in formulating the stages through which instrumental music has passed, according to a development theory as applied to music, considers the drum first responded to the nascent conception of music in the prehistoric man, and has since been tenaciously preserved as an adjunct to religious service among partially civilised races. The Nautch girls, at "India in London," London, 1886, performed their soothing gyrations to the gentle Sárungí, a bowed instrument with sympathetic strings, accompanied by the beating of such drums.

There are many varieties of drums to be found in India, the names varying in different parts of the country. The largest of the three Drums here shown is not used by professional musicians, but in bands of street music found in all bazaars, and over the gateways of temples, etc., called Nahabat, or Nakkera Khaneh (in South India, Perya méla), and composed of low-class Mahomedans, or Hindus of the barber caste. Such bands consist of drums of various shapes and kinds, and primitive instruments of the oboe kind, with drones and cymbals. Musicians in the East are usually placed over the gateways, nearly all of importance having galleries for that purpose.

Professional musicians and Nautch girls generally use the *M'ridang* or *Tabla*. The Drum with the striped body and leather braces is a kind of M'ridang. The genuine Drum bearing this name is longer in proportion to its diameter, and has one head larger than the other. The two heads are tuned to the tonic and fourth or fifth as required. The pieces of wood between the braces and shell are used to assist in the tuning, and should be noticed. *Tabla* are small copper kettledrums tuned similarly. Drum-playing upon such instruments is a great art, and can only be learned by years of study. A good *Tabla* or *M'ridang* player will earn from 100 to 150 rupees per month. The wrist, flat of the hand, and fingers are employed. Such instruments should not be very noisy, the skill of the player being the first consideration. The M'ridang is considered to be the most ancient of Indian Drums; its origin is popularly ascribed to the god Mahadeo (S'iva).

The earthenware Kettledrum or Tam-Tam, here shown, is used by beggars and fakirs to attract attention as they wander from house to house. A similarly shaped kettledrum of copper, but very much larger—about three or four feet in diameter—is known by the name of Nagara or Nakkera, and is much used in the bands attached to the service of temples, and found over the gates of forts and palaces of native chiefs. Such drums are beaten in a peculiar way with short curved sticks; and, although when heard close the sound is anything but pleasing, yet, when heard from a distance among the mountains, in company with shrill oboes and deeper drones, the sounds rising and falling with the breeze and echoing from hill to hill, the effect is in character with the wildness of the country, and the hearer often listens, rapt, in spite of himself.

The three Drums, here represented, belong to the Music Class Room of the University of Edinburgh, and have been drawn by the permission of Professor Sir Herbert Oakeley.

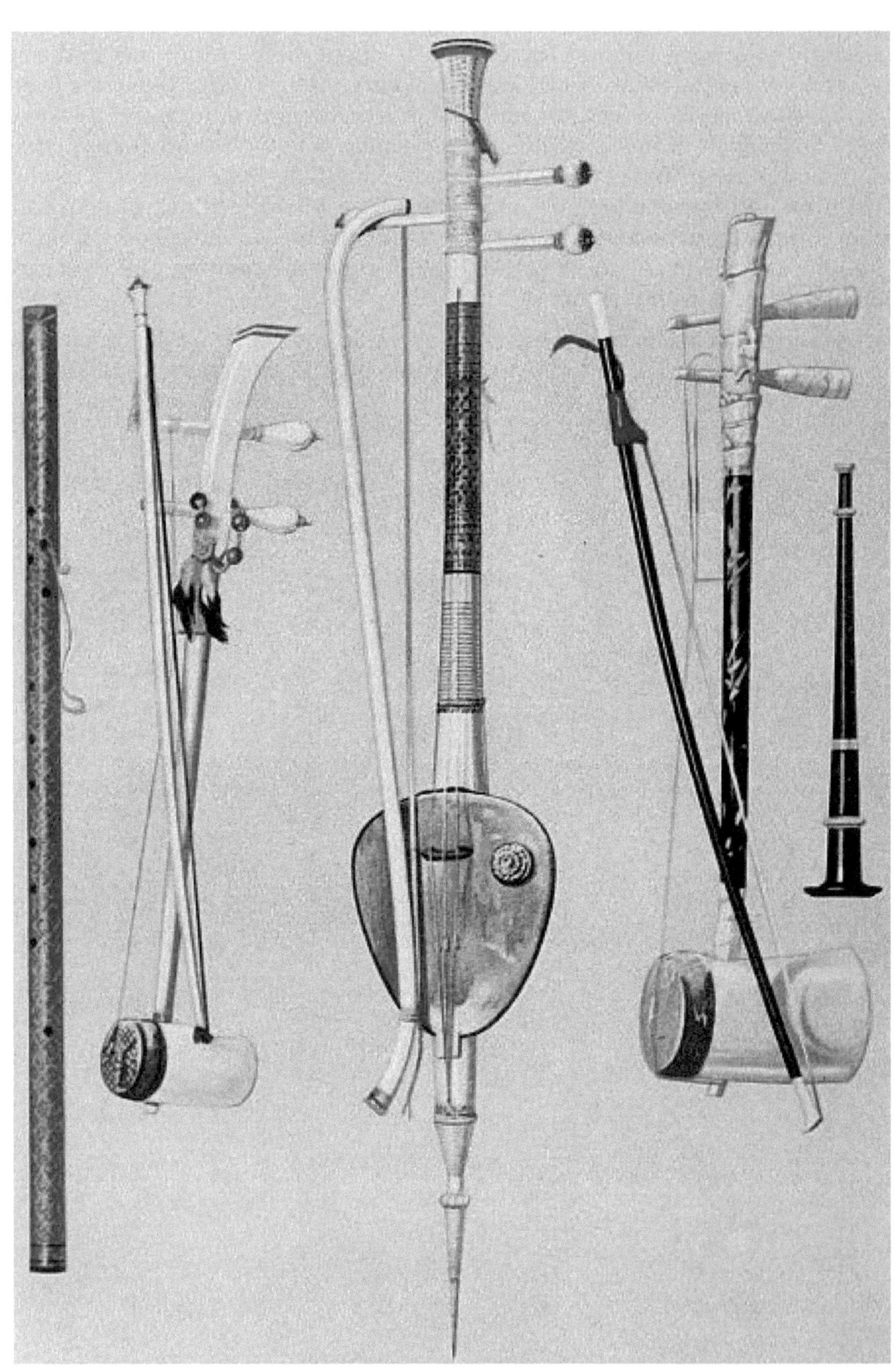

Plate XLII.

PLATE XLII.

SAW DUANG & BOW. SAW TAI & BOW. SAW OO & BOW. KLUI. PEE.

HESE instruments belong to H.M. the King of Siam, and were drawn by the gracious permission of H.R.H. Prince Narés Varariddhi, then Siamese Minister in England, and brother of the King.

The Saw Tai, or Siamese fiddle (centre figure), has the lower part of the neck of carved ivory, and the upper part of gold enamelled. The back is of cocoa-nut shells, jewelled. There is a jewelled boss on the sound membrane, which is of parchment. It is the same instrument as the Javese Rabáb, and is of Persian origin. The strings, three in number, of silk cord, meet at the top beneath the pegs, and pass under a ligature, whence they diverge to the bridge. It has no finger-board, and the length of string to vibrate is not marked off, as is usual with bowed instruments, by pressure upon the finger-board, but by pressing the independent string with the entire width of the finger, which leaves the intonation a little uncertain. The player squats cross-legged, and holds the instrument in a sloping position.

The Saw Chine, or Chinese fiddle, is shown in two varieties, the Saw Duang (left of centre figure) with jewels round one of the pegs, and the Saw Oo (right of centre figure). Like the Saw Tai, these fiddles have no finger-boards. The bow-string, as in the Chinese Urh-hsien and Hu-ch'in, is inserted between the strings so as to play either. The wind instruments here shown are a Klui, or flute (on the left), which has a membrane over one hole, resembling the Basque galoubet; and the Pee (on the right), a kind of oboe, very harsh, and resembling in tone a very powerful bagpipe, a resemblance assisted by the peculiar heptatonic scale of the Siamese, being not far off the Syrian scale, noticed in the Scotch bagpipe. (See Introduction, page xv., and Plates V. and XLIII.) The Pee is considered to be of Javese origin.

There are four kinds of Bands in Siam, the precise details of which are given in *Notes on Siamese Musical Instruments*, a work prepared at the Siamese Embassy and published in London, 1885. The Lao Phān Band, peculiar to the north of Siam, includes the reed instrument called Phān, mentioned in the Introduction, page xvii.

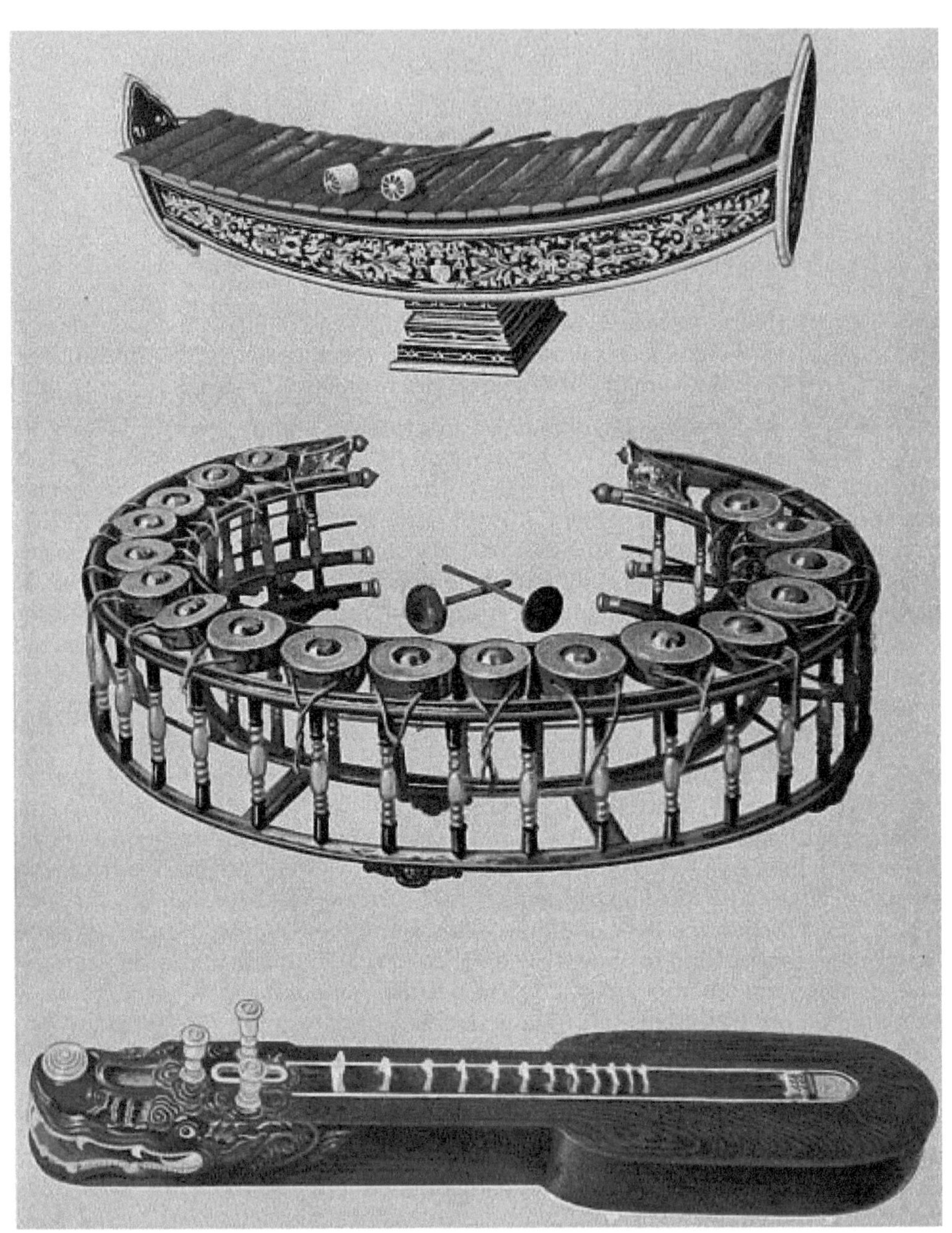

Plate XLIII.

PLATE XLIII.

RANAT EK. KHONG YAI. TA'KHAY.

THESE instruments, like those drawn in Plate XLII., belong to H.M. the King of Siam, and were also drawn for this work by the gracious permission of H.R.H. Prince Narés.

Harmonicons of wood and of metal, such as the Ranat and Khong, are the foundation of music in Siam, Burma, Java, and the Indian Archipelago generally. They also extend into India, and even, in another direction, to South Africa. Tuned in Siam to a heptatonic scale, not founded upon an harmonic conception of chords, they present, at least ideally, a ladder of seven equal steps, with which the native ear is satisfied. The performances, some years ago, of the King of Siam's band in the Royal Albert Hall, South Kensington, allowed this scale to be heard, and afforded full scope to the remarkable technical skill of the Ranat players.

The instruments drawn are a Ranat Ek of twenty-one wooden bars, in a cradle-like stand beautifully ornamented with ivory; a Khong Yai of eighteen metal kettles, of a kind of bronze or bell metal known as "gongsa," in an ivory stand painted like tortoise-shell, with brass edgings; and the very peculiar Ta'khay, or crocodile, with three strings and twelve bridges, including the nut, to fret them. The last-mentioned instrument is played with a plectrum, and ornamented with a crocodile's head and ivory ornaments.

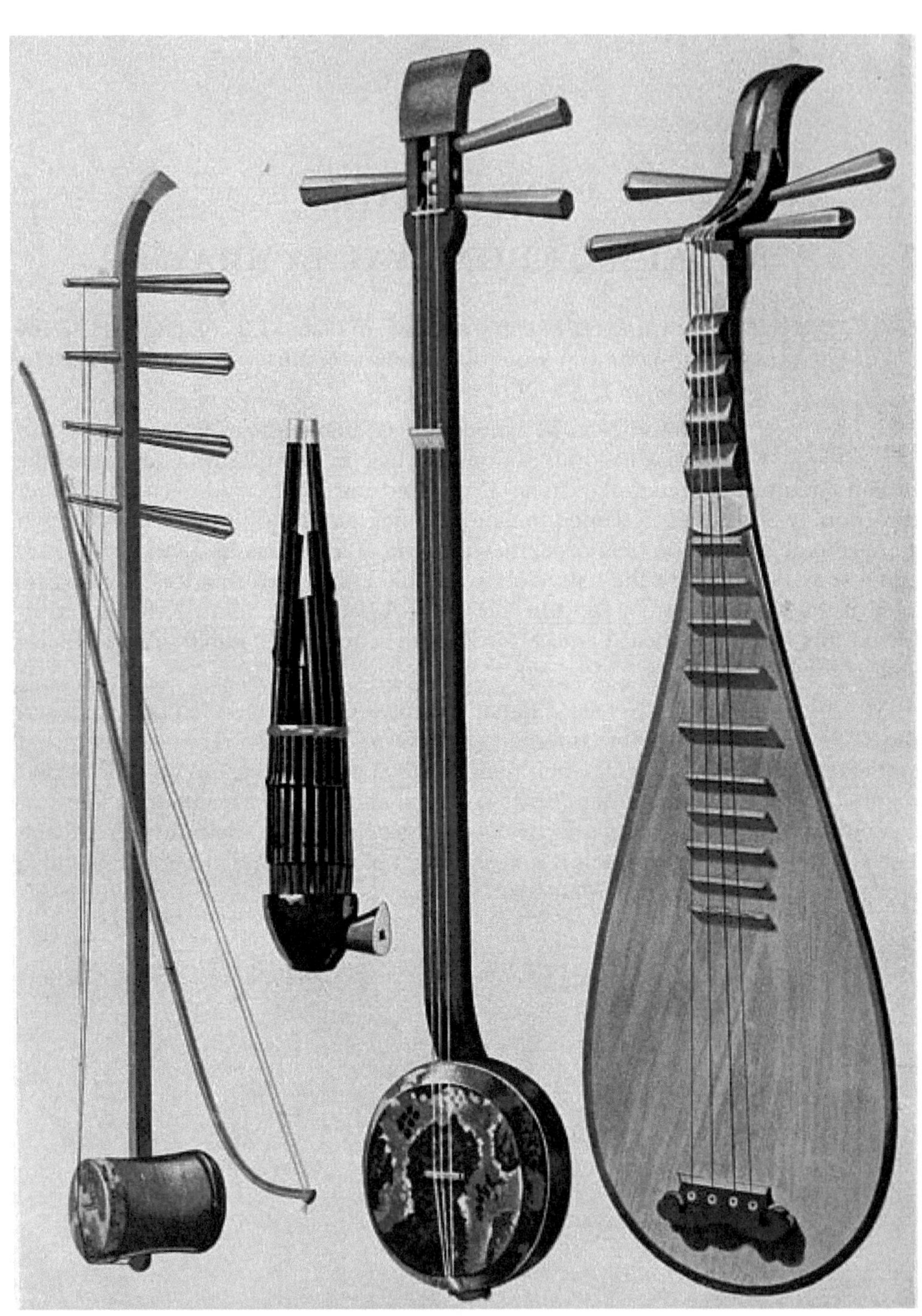

Plate XLIV.

PLATE XLIV.

HU-CH'IN & BOW. SHÊNG. SAN-HSIEN. P'I-P'A.

E learn from Mr. J.A. Van Aalst's comprehensive treatise on Chinese Music, published, it may at first sight appear somewhat oddly, by the Imperial Maritime Customs (Shanghai, 1884), that the Hu-ch'in, the left-hand figure in the Plate, is one of the most popular musical instruments in Peking. The strings, four in number, are of silk, and are tuned in pairs a fifth apart. This instrument is in fact a double-strung Erh-hsien or Urh-hsien (Van Aalst and Dennys; Ur-heen, Engel), and has the same peculiar arrangement by which the bow is fixed between the strings for playing. It is of cane and horsehair, and the rosin for it is stuck upon the body, a hollow cylinder of bamboo, wood, or copper, through which the long neck of the instrument is thrust. The upper end of the body is covered with snakeskin, while the lower is left open. The Erh-hsien, which has a similar bamboo body but two strings only, is more generally popular than the Hu-ch'in, and is met with all over China. The Ti-ch'in, according to Dennys the favourite instrument with blind men, is also similarly bowed, and has half a cocoa-nut shell for the body, covered by a thin board. These bowed instruments, it is believed, found their way into China with the Buddhist religion.

The name for the next instrument, the reed mouth-organ, Shêng, sounds like "shung," rhyming with "sung." From this ancient instrument have come the modern popular developments of the "free-reed" organ, first applied about 1780, at the instance of Professor Kratzenstein, to organ reed-stops by a Copenhagen organ-builder named Kirsnick, who had settled at St. Petersburg, an invention soon afterwards carried to Germany by the celebrated Abbé Vogler. The French Harmonium and American Organ, the concertinas and accordion, are well-known examples of the "free-reed" principle, which differs from the Church organ beating-reed inasmuch as the reed or vibrator of metal does not overlap any part of its frame. The Shêng is a gourd with its top cut off and a flat cover cemented upon it. Twenty-one bamboo pipes are inserted round the cover, but four, being intended for convenience in holding the instrument, do not sound. Those intended to sound are provided with small brass reeds. By a peculiar arrangement, unique in reed instruments, the wind, attacking all the reeds simultaneously, at once escapes by ventages in the pipes, until stopped by the fingers for the pipes that are to sound. The lengths of the pipes are merely ornamental, the actual lengths required being determined by slot-like cuttings in the pipes, not seen in front. There are seventeen sounding pipes, as already said, but only eleven notes, as some notes are repeated in the unison or octave. The scale, which the *à peu près* musicians are satisfied with, may be thus noted—

The succession of notes in the first octave resembles that of the ancient Phrygian mode and that church mode in which Thomas Tallis's famous service is composed. The exact measurements of the intervals heard at the Health Exhibition are to be found in Mr. A.J. Ellis's Paper *On the Musical Scales of Various Nations,* published in the *Journal of the Society of Arts,* London, 25th March, 1885.

Mr. N.B. Dennys, in his valuable notes on Chinese Musical Instruments read before the North China Branch of the Asiatic Society, 21st October, 1873, gives the name of the three-stringed instrument in the drawing, with a long neck like a tamboura, as San-hsien, with which Mr. Van Aalst agrees. The Peking musicians called it Sien-tzê (pronounced like Shen-zy). Like the Japanese Siamisen the San-hsien has no frets. The drum-like body is covered on the upper side with snakeskin, the under side being left open as in a tambourine or banjo. The three strings were tuned ascending a minor tone between the first and second, and a fifth between the second and third strings: the outer strings being consequently a major sixth apart. The strings were plucked by two bone plectra extended like claws beyond the ends of the fingers, and the player stopped a Pentatonic or five-note scale, thus:

nearly in just intonation.

The P'i-p'a, according to Dennys and Van Aalst, or Balloon Guitar (the Peking musicians called it Phi-pe), has a body nearly a foot in diameter, from which it takes its English name, and four strings played usually with the fingers and tuned as fourth, fifth, and octave from the lowest note. The large semi-elliptical frets above the finger-board were not used by the player at the Health Exhibition; he restricted himself to the twelve frets upon the finger-board. The P'i-p'a is usually played by men who, in the South of China, are hired as minstrels or ballad-singers. The stopping of this instrument was pentatonic, as with the San-hsien, and the scale began upon the same note, but the tuning of the fretted instrument was less good than that noted of the unfretted one. Mr. Van Aalst informs us that the notes are reiterated by rapidly passing the long finger-nail or plectrum backwards and forwards across the string, to produce an effect of sostenuto similarly sought for in Europe for the Mandoline, Bandurria, and Dulcimer. These instruments belong to the Music Class Room of the University of Edinburgh.

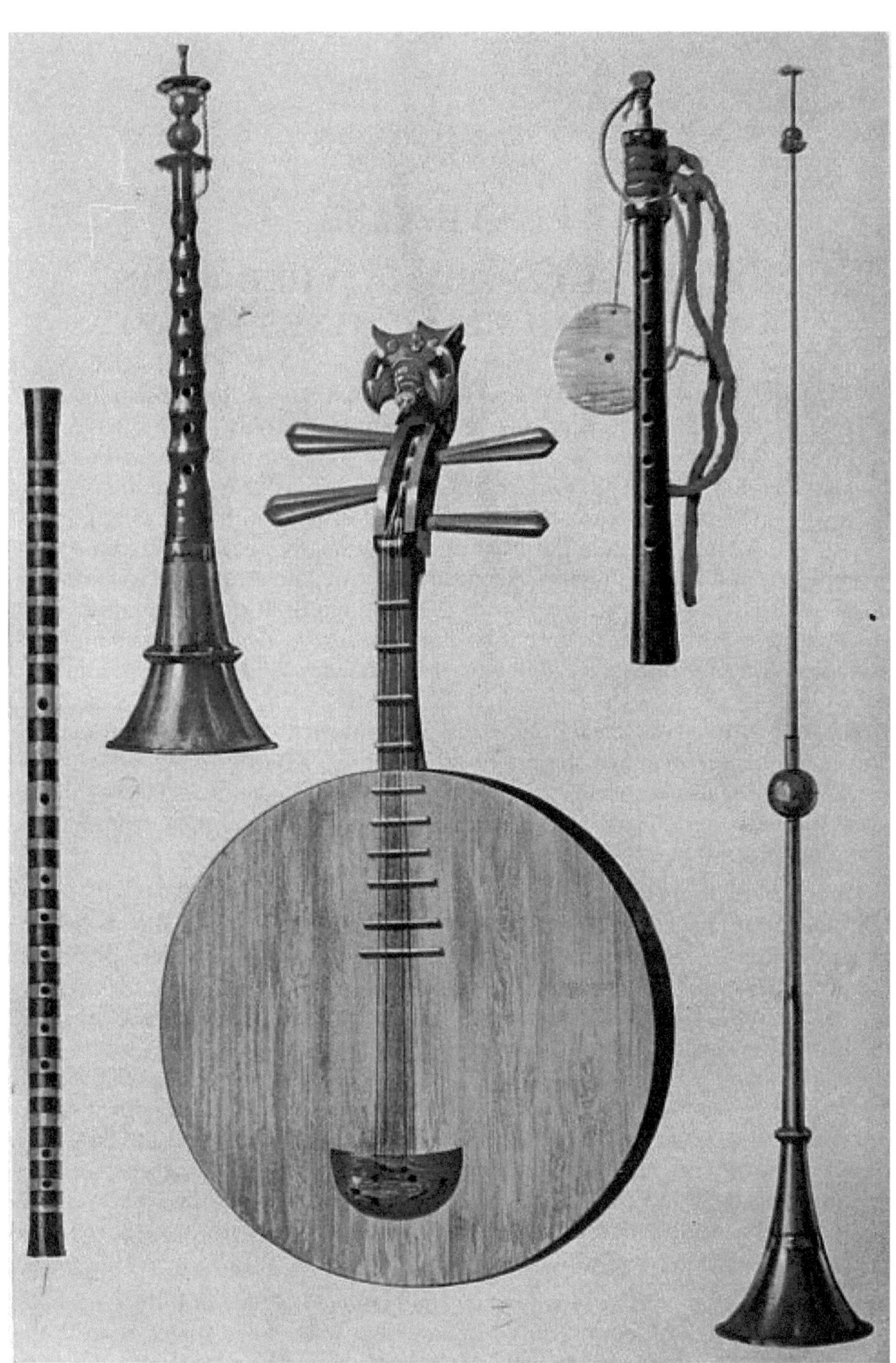

Plate XLV.

PLATE XLV.

CHINESE TI-TZU, SO-NA, YUEH-CH'IN. JAPANESE HIJI-RIKI. CHINESE LA-PA.

HE Ti-tzu to the left in the Plate is the Chinese flute. It is usually bound round with waxed silk and ornamented with tassels. It has seven holes besides the embouchure, that nearest to the latter being covered with a thin membrane as in the Provençal galoubet, taken from the sap of the bamboo and melted at the moment it is applied, intended to make the quality of tone more reedy. The remaining six holes are stopped by the fingers. According to Mr. Van Aalst, twelve notes in a diatonic succession, beginning upon the A of the violin, form the compass of this instrument, but with much uncertainty of intonation, which may be as much due to the measuring for boring by the instrument-makers as to the peculiarities of an ideal Chinese scale. The scale played at the Health Exhibition, South Kensington, in 1884, by a native ti-tzu player, was a B flat scale with the third rather sharper than the minor but less than the major third, that is, a neuter third, which, as we have seen, is frequently met with in Eastern non-harmonic scales. However, there is great difficulty in determining wind instrument scales accurately, from the power the player has to alter intonation by blowing differently.

The Chinese So-na is a copper wind instrument—a kind of oboe—played with a double reed. On account of the shortness of the reed there is a disk below it to protect the lips of the player. There are two small pierced copper spheres like those in the trumpets in Fra Angelico's paintings, beneath which are the seven finger-holes in the front and two thumb-holes behind the pipe. A loose brass cone of considerable size covers the lower end and is fastened to the upper by a string. This instrument is possibly the Indian Soonai. There are nine notes, as in the Scotch bagpipe, which the So-na somewhat resembles in quality of tone, but it is more strident and disagreeable. The scale, as played by a native at the Health Exhibition, gave intervals of whole and three-quarter tones resembling the bagpipe, but as the performer succeeded in playing with other instruments that apparently differed in scale, the accommodation in blowing must be credited with the approximately satisfactory result.

The Yueh-ch'in, or Moon Guitar, so called from the shape of the sound-board, has four silk strings tuned as fifths in pairs. The strings are struck with the finger-nails, which the Chinese wear long, or a plectrum. The strings are sometimes of copper instead of silk. The instrument is chiefly used to accompany the voice, and the repetition of a note, as in the P'i-p'a, appears to be a favourite effect.

The next wind instrument in Plate XLV. is the Japanese Hiji-riki, a conical pipe with a double reed inserted in the larger end. From this cause the instrument sounds about an octave lower than a pipe that is cylindrical. The Hiji-riki is of bamboo, the interior being covered with a bed of red lacquer. It has seven finger-holes and two thumb-holes at the back. The scale, as given by Mr. Victor Mahillon, from whose *Catalogue Descriptif et Analytique du Musée Instrumental du Conservatoire Royal de Bruxelles,* I have been glad to borrow, here and elsewhere, is diatonic, with the occasional insertion of a sharp fourth. This interval is frequently heard in Chinese music, when there are ascending seven-note scales. The disk suspended at the top of the pipe is adjusted, when the Hiji-riki is played, to protect the player's lips—a precaution due to the shortness of the metal reed.

The long trumpet is the Chinese La-pa, with a sliding tube on the trombone principle. It gives four notes, the octave, twelfth, super-octave, and seventeenth, but not the prime. As may be imagined, it is a military instrument, but Mr. Van Aalst informs us it is a privilege of itinerant knife-grinders to blow it in the streets to announce their whereabouts. A La-pa, with the bell bent back, is used at wedding processions.

The instruments drawn in this Plate belong to the Music Class Room of Edinburgh University.

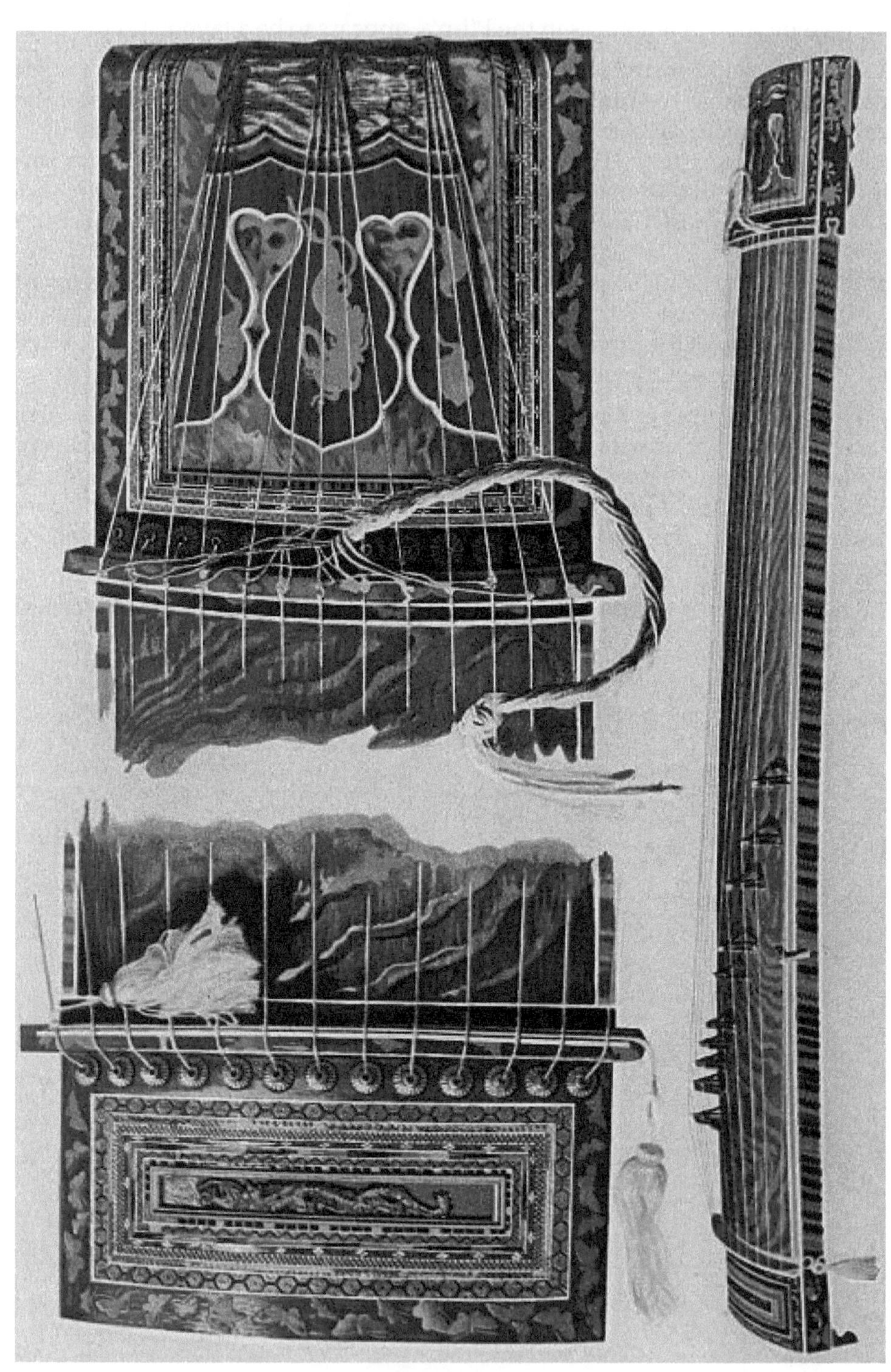

Plate XLVI.

PLATE XLVI.

JAPANESE KOTO.

THIS is the thirteen-stringed Sono Koto of Japan, and a very beautifully-ornamented specimen, lent for drawing by Mr. George Wood, of Messrs. Cramer and Co., Regent Street, London.

The strings of the koto are, as in all Japanese stringed instruments, of silk drawn through wax, and the accordance follows the pentatonic system already described in connection with the Siamisen, and as given by Mr. Isawa, Director of the Institute of Music at Tokio, in twelve different popular pentatonic accordances, which are the foundations for, but, as will be explained, do not exactly fix the intervals of the koto player's performances. The strings are equally long and thick, and are strained to one tension, the notes being obtained by means of movable bridges, of which there are as many as there are strings. Two strings, the first and third, are tuned alike, at the interval of a fifth above the second or lowest note. The tuning is generally done by ear note by note, the player pitching the instrument to his voice, which is good if a high voice. The classical Japanese music is Chinese, and may have come to Japan with Chinese art, through the Corea. It is, however, only played in the Imperial household or the Shinto temples. Both classical and popular music are pentatonic, but the Japanese in no way avoid semitones, which give the Chinese so much trouble when they endeavour to produce them. The koto player, in performing, squats very low upon the ground, and wears plectra-like wire thimbles on the right hand, terminating in small projections of ivory, touching with them only the shorter division of the strings. He has, however, the power, by pressing down the longer unsounded lengths with the ends of the fingers of the left hand, or pulling them towards the bridges, to increase and decrease the tension of the strings, and thus sharpen or flatten the notes and modify the tuning by intermediate tones—a licence not used unsparingly. The Japanese pictures of koto players invariably show this practice. The dimensions of this Koto are, approximately: length, 6 feet 2½ inches; width, 8¾ to 9¾ inches; depth, about 1¾ inches at the sides. The instrument is made of strong Kiri wood, and has two openings on the under side. The beauty of the ornament of the instrument drawn could hardly be surpassed. The drawing shows enlargements of the two ends, one half the actual size, and displays the highly decorative adornment of this remarkable instrument.

The favourite popular tuning of the Koto is called Hira-dioshi. It is thus given by Mr. Isawa and other authorities:—

The music-master at the Japanese Village, Knightsbridge, London, tuned the Koto to a Siamisen (Plate XLVII.), with the pentatonic intervals marked on the neck according to a peculiarity of intonation referred to in the description of that instrument.

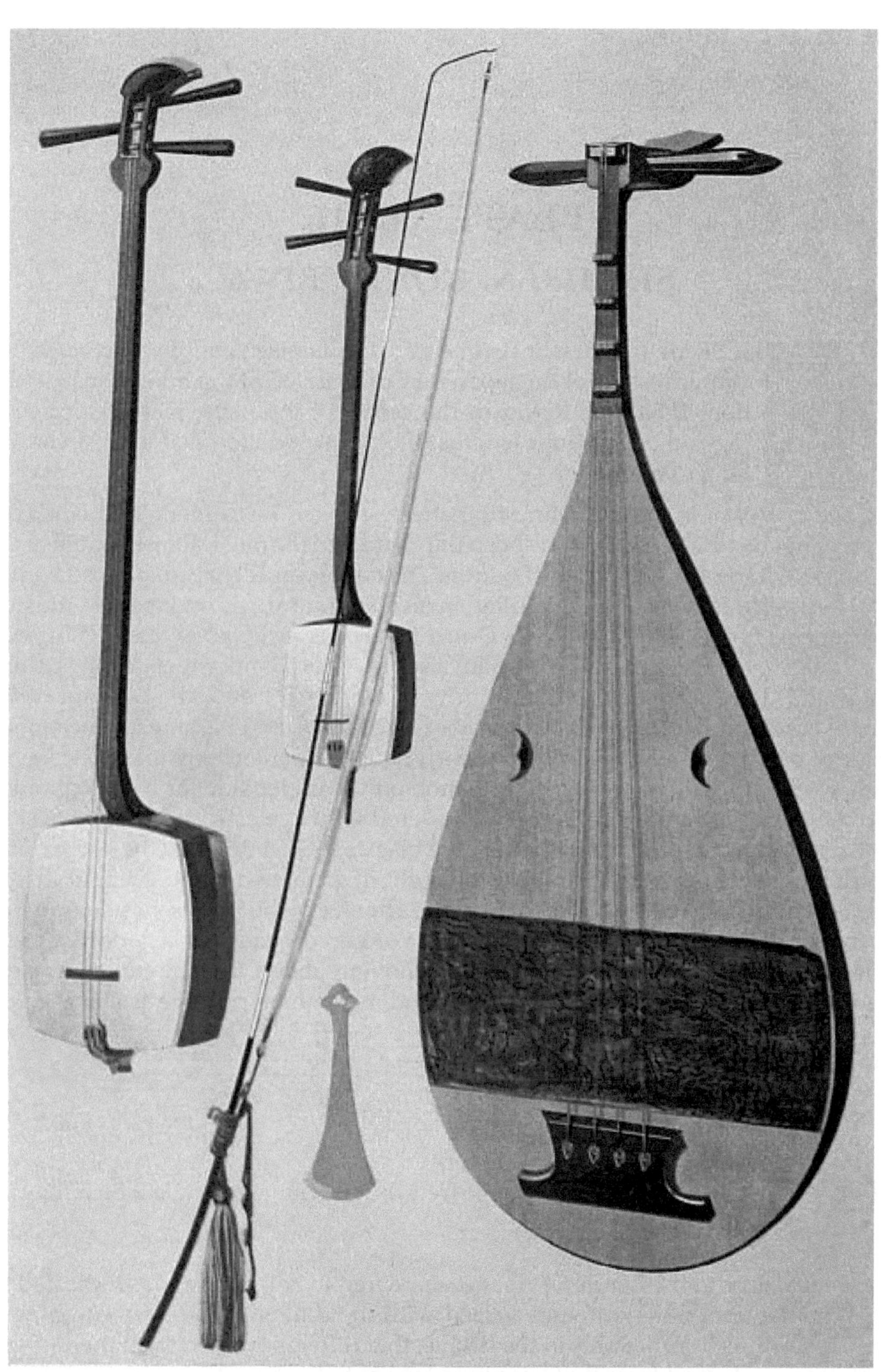

Plate XLVII.

PLATE XLVII.

SIAMISEN, KOKIU, BIWA.

HESE are Japanese instruments. The Siamisen and Biwa were drawn by permission of the Japanese Commission of the Inventions Exhibition, 1885. The Kokiu in the centre of the plate, and its long fishing-rod bow in four lengths of black wood mounted with silver, belong to the writer.

The Siamisen is the commonest Japanese stringed instrument, and is played by the singing girls (Gesha); it has been the characteristic musical instrument at the Japanese Village, Knightsbridge, London. The name was there pronounced Samiseng (the *a* as in father), and Dr. Müller, in an elaborate article on Japanese musical instruments in the *Mittheilungen der Deutschen Gesellschaft für Natur und Völkerkunde Ostasien's*, 6tes Heft. (Berlin, 1884), invariably writes Samiseng, but the spelling Siamisen is here adopted on the authority of Mr. Shuji Isawa, the Director of the School of Music, Tokio. In length it is about 37 inches, and has a resonance membrane of parchment stretched upon a nearly square wooden body that is 7½ inches high, 6½ wide, and 3 deep. There is a knob on the under side for a string holder, and the upper and under sides of it are covered with a selected part of a cat's skin, on which the bridge also rests. By the little black spots on this skin the value of the instrument is determined. Four give the highest value; two mark ordinary instruments; while those without spots are cheap. The size of the Siamisen is determined by the singer's voice. Good voices are high voices; consequently a good singer requires a smaller one. For convenience in moving about, the body and neck are made to separate. It has three silk strings and in common practice as many accordances, viz. , and . It is without frets, but the fingered scale which the Japanese musicians at the London "village" appeared to know only, was indicated by small marks upon the neck, and agreed with the tuning of the thirteen-stringed koto. It has thus five intervals in the octave, that differ, however, from the Chinese pentatonic scale, and from that known in Java as Salendro. The Japanese, as heard at the "village," may be described, when descending, as a major third, a semitone, a neuter or mean third (neither major nor minor, but equivalent to a three-quarter tone and a whole tone), thus  —the × denoting the mean third. This was accepted as right by natives of various parts of Japan brought together in the village whose speech dialects were not the same, although their musical dialect was thus uniform. However, since Mr. Isawa gives the interval as a minor third, and in performances which I have heard the minor effect certainly predominates, I am disposed to accept the mean third here recorded as only a widening of the normal minor third. Great latitude has to be allowed in dealing with scales, especially those of non-harmonic origin. Our own equal temperament narrowing of the same interval is rarely noticed by us, and passes as a matter of course. The Siamisen is employed to accompany the dancing and singing women, and its tones are an important aid to the effect of their performance.

The plectrum of the Siamisen is called in Japanese Batsi. It is shown in the plate.

The Kokiu is a kind of fiddle, in its construction very like the Siamisen, only that it is played with a bow (kiu) instead of a plectrum or striker (batsi). It is usually a woman's instrument, but is now very little played. Dr. Müller only heard one player in Tokio, a blind man, from whom he took his description of the instrument and the manner of performance. The whole length of the Kokiu is about 25 inches, the body being 5 inches long and broad. It is 2½ inches deep and covered like the Siamisen. Instead of the string-holder of the latter it has a 2½ inch long round metal slip to which the strings are knotted. The bridge is long and very low, with notches to receive the strings; three being equally spaced, while the fourth is very near the third. The strings are tuned , the two near each other being unisons of the highest note. The bow is 45 inches long, of four lengths as already mentioned. It takes to pieces for transport. It is flat behind and oval in front. It is bent at the top nearly to a right angle, and the whole rod is very elastic. It is strung with white horsehair about 32 inches long, the horsehair being imported, as there is no long horsehair in Japan. It is fastened with a silken knot into a silver holder. In order to play the Kokiu the bow is taken with the thumb, middle, and little fingers, the index finger being extended along the back. With stretched-out fourth finger the player strains the slack hair of the bow, then takes up the instrument, vertically resting it upon the knees, between which the metal string-holder is grasped. Bringing the hair of the bow to the edge of the resonance body, the bow is simply moved horizontally backwards and forwards, the middle part of the bowstring only being employed. The strings are brought into contact with the bow by a rotary movement of the instrument. Sometimes only one E flat string is used, sometimes both. Double notes are very rarely used. The sound of the Kokiu is very like that of the Hurdy-Gurdy, but much weaker in comparison.

The Biwa is a lute-like instrument in the shape of a divided pear, becoming narrower upwards. The body is about 34 inches long, of which 7½ come on to the finger-board. There are four frets on the finger-board. It has four strings in two thicknesses tuned, according to Dr. Müller, prime, quint, octave, tenth, like an infantry bugle, but Dr. Isawa gives no less than six accordances. The Biwa is played with a bill-formed batsi 6½ inches long, made of horn, wood, tortoiseshell, or ivory.

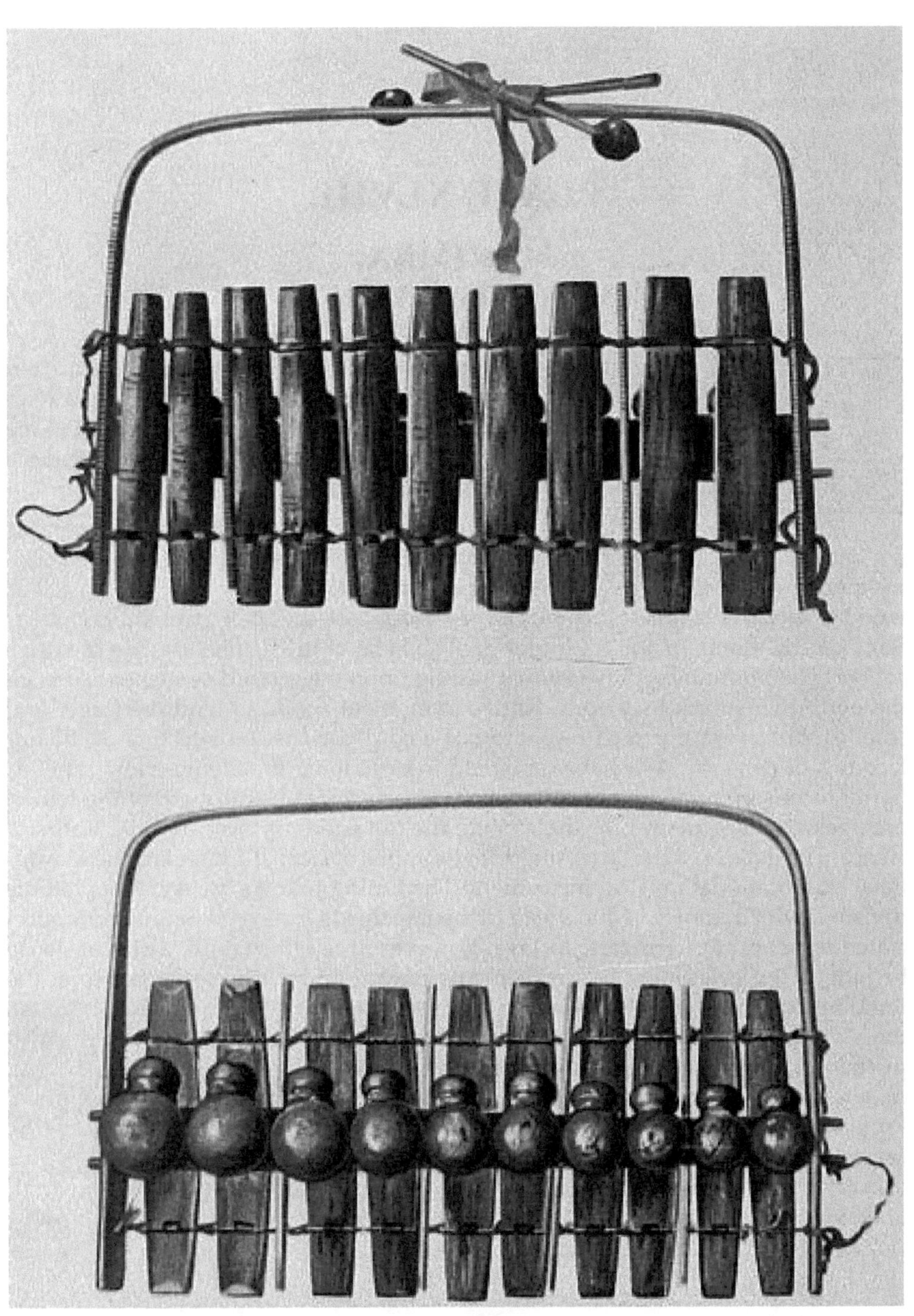

Plate XLVIII.

PLATE XLVIII.

MARIMBA, OF SOUTH AFRICA.

A ZULU harmonicon in two views, the back and front. There are ten bars, each with a gourd resonator attached to it. It is played with drumsticks, one in each hand. This Marimba was presented to me by Mr. John Robertson, of Durban, Natal, and he has furnished the following details respecting it.

The Zulu name, Marimba, is varied by Izambilo; the former is the better known. This instrument is made by the Mindonga tribe, whose country marches with the Portuguese settlement of Inhambane on the East Coast. The wood of the bars is called Intzari. The resonators are the shell of a fruit known as Strychnos M'Kenii, or the Kafir orange. The balls of the drumsticks are of native rubber. The Marimba is played either resting upon the ground or suspended from the performer's neck by a cord. Native gum is employed to bind the larger and smaller shells forming each resonator. The cord used is the intestine of the aulacodus, or cane rat. As I have remarked in describing the Siamese instruments, harmonicons of wood and metal are very widely spread—throughout the Indian archipelago, in Siam and Burma, among the hill tribes of India and the Kafirs of Africa. The natives of the little American Republic of Costa Rica regard the Marimba as their national musical instrument. The tuning follows the equal heptatonic division, which allows of the mean or neuter thirds, ruling in Siam, and appreciated by many Eastern ears. In Java, however, it is not so; and, as far as could be judged, by examining the instruments played on by the native Javese at the London Aquarium in 1882 (other instruments apparently gave different results), there are two distinct Javese tunings,—the one, called Salendro, an ideally equal pentatonic, or five interval scale in the octave, the other, called Pelog, a heptatonic, or seven interval scale in the octave, the law of which has not been determined. From the latter are selected sets of five notes to form pentatonic scales, presenting remarkable differences.

INDEX.

E

F

G

H

I

J

K

L

M

N

O

P

Q

R

S

T

U

V

W

9 789361 382376

Printed by Libri Plureos GmbH in Hamburg,
Germany